D0981974

8|11

How to Use
What You've
GOT
to get
What You
WANT

Advanced Praise for

How to Use
What You've Got
to Get What You Want

"As Marilyn Tam makes eminently clear, what are you waiting for? When you have an opportunity to learn from a book written by a successful, minority businesswoman and humanitarian, who had every excuse not to make it in corporate America, take it! Marilyn's credentials speak for themselves, but most important, her guidelines and stories will help you get started now on living the life that you were meant to live, with work you truly enjoy."

— MARK S. ALBION, PH.D.,
author of the *New York Times* bestseller,
Making a Life, Making a Living; former
Harvard Business School professor; *Fortune* 500 consultant;
and successful entrepreneur

"Marilyn Tam is more than a successful businesswoman and entrepreneur. She has a mission to make this world a better place. Her message in this fabulous, accessible book is that each one of us has a mission and a gift to share. By starting from where we are, using what we already have, we can manifest our dreams. This book is a course in practical magic. Use it and let yourself fly."

— JOAN BORYSENKO, PH.D.,
author of numerous *New York Times* bestsellers, including
Inner Peace for Busy People; cofounder and former director of the
Mind Body clinics at the Harvard teaching hospitals,
Beth Israel/Deaconess Medical Center

"A very important contribution to the art of living a successful, happy, fulfilled life especially in the complicated, highly competitive world of business. I left marking slips on the sides of the pages to return to them."

— ROBERT MULLER,
2002 Nobel Peace Prize nominee,
Assistant Secretary General of The United Nations for 30 years

"What do you get when you cross an altruistic nature with top-level responsibilities at Reebok, Nike, Aveda, and Britannia? This book! Marilyn Tam brings elegant theories down to earth with devastatingly effective checklists for success. Some business books inspire and others guide, but few backup their visions with itemized formulas for specific accomplishments. With insight, grace, and wisdom Marilyn Tam's book proves that enlightenment can have its commercial rewards."

— JIM MULLEN,
founder and former CEO of Mullen Advertising,
and former Vice Chairman of The Lowe Group,
a division of The Interpublic Group of Companies,
a $7.2 billion global marketing communications
and marketing services company

"The wisdom of this book was obtained by true knowledge, which is gained through experience. Marilyn Tam has mastered the art of business by living it. This book will help anyone become an achiever if they follow Marilyn's brilliance."

— HORST M. RECHELBACHER,
Founder, Aveda Corporation

"This book rings true! At Ben & Jerry's we're able to combine three things—innovative, high-quality products; economic success; and social change. Marilyn Tam's book fulfills on all three criteria. It's a fabulous tool for anyone who is interested in finding and fulfilling their life purpose. Marilyn's remarkable business experience, common sense, and humor distinguish her Principles and blueprint from others on how to flourish in the world and in your personal life. I heartily recommend it."

— BEN COHEN,
Cofounder, Ben & Jerry's Homemade, Inc.

"Marilyn Tam is an extraordinary woman who possesses a unique sense of business leadership. The intuition and practical experience that Marilyn shares through How to Use What You've Got to Get What You Want *is a testament to her innate ability to motivate and inspire others. This book is an excellent tool for anyone seeking to make a difference in their personal or professional lives. It provides easy to use strategies and practical guidelines, which empowers the*

reader to look within and utilize their own potential. I highly recommend this book to anyone on their quest for fulfillment through their mission."

— PAMELA CHALOULT,
CoExecutive Director, Social Venture Network

"Marilyn Tam has revealed a precise and practical method of manifesting our heart's desire. With a refined clarity she has identified Principles and practices that work in the world to fulfill our life's purpose. A brilliant work, which I highly recommend."

— BARBARA MARX HUBBARD,
visionary futurist, author, social architect, spiritual pioneer,
and President, Foundation for Conscious Evolution

"A unique book that brings spirituality into materialism and shows us how the two can complement each other. A must read for all potential and present corporate executives. I found it equally useful in the nonprofit arena; the insights and advice apply there also. I highly recommend this book!"

— ARUN GANDHI,
renowned international peace leader, author, teacher,
speaker, and Founder/Executive Director of
M.K. Gandhi Institute for Nonviolence

"This is a book for the "can do" folks to fulfill all our dreams and potential! With commonsensical wisdom and no-nonsense clarity, Marilyn has given us a brilliant and simple guidebook to explore the human journey. Excellently done. Bravo!"

— CHUNGLIANG AL HUANG,
founder and President of the Living Tao Foundation,
and author of *Embrace Tiger, Return to Mountain*

"We certainly need books and speakers who do encourage people to believe in themselves, and the potential of their lives. This is more than that, for it instructs people how to accomplish their goals. This is extremely well-done, and effective. It is like a road map, how to get from here to there. [Marilyn Tam] fills the book with interesting and perceptive observations, and reminds all of us of the basic approach

we must make to the challenges we face. I am a true believer in what [she] says, and [she] says it very well. I love the way [she] shares [her] personal experience. This is the most important part of inspiring others to believe in the possible."

— DAVID WINTER PH.D.,
Director of the American Council on Education's Commission on Women in Higher Education, Director of the Association of Presidents of Independent Colleges and Universities, Chancellor at Westmont College, California

"Take your passion and make it happen with this powerful book filled with the essential tools for your rapid success in any business or situation. I loved your work, every page filled with wisdom!"

— BARBARA GAUGHEN,
author and President of Gaughen Global Promotions

"I was captivated by your book. There are so many useful ideas, I keep thinking of all the people I know who would benefit from and enjoy your book. It is extremely well-written. I loved it; I wouldn't say this to a fellow writer if I didn't honestly mean it. Congratulations, well done."

— CHARLES MCPHEE, A.K.A. "THE DREAM DOCTOR,"
author of *Ask the Dream Doctor*, radio personality, resident dream expert on AOL.com, and Oxygen, and national radio personality on Cox radio

"A must read! Brilliant, inspiring insight for leaders! Companies have paid millions for this kind of coaching and now it's available to everyone. These ideas will ripple throughout business for the next decade. Be the first to bring them into your company."

— KATE LUDEMAN, PH.D.,
President, Worth Ethic Corporation, and author of *The Corporate Mystic* (with Gay Hendricks)

"It is often said that the real truths are simple; it's the execution that is difficult. In this book the execution is simple because the truths are so authentic. The stories, laced with insight, weave an empowering personal leadership formula that is applicable to any situation and every person. You will want this book to know the magnitude of

what you have and with the very act of reading it you will become a creative leader in your life and in your work."

— EDDIE ERLANDSON, M.D.,
coauthor of *Radical Change, Radical Results*
(with Kate Ludeman), former Chief of Staff of
St. Joseph Mercy Hospital, and founder of
Life Lessons Wellness Program

"Marilyn Tam is a true visionary. Her most profound accomplishments lie beyond the normal hallmarks of being a successful businesswoman, and can be found in her deep wisdom, remarkable clarity, and generosity of spirit. How to Use What You've Got to Get What You Want *is more than just a powerful guide for dreamers and doers—it is an infusion of inspiration and encouragement that will uplift any reader and make him or her grateful to have read this wonderful book."*

— BARBARA DE ANGELIS, PH.D.,
New York Times bestselling author, TV personality,
Motivational Speaker, and Human Relations expert

"The magic of this book begins in the first few pages and unfolds Marilyn's four guiding principles. At last a guide, written by someone who has actually been there, making it easy for anyone who wants to take the next leaps!""

— PATTY DEDOMINIC,
Founder and CEO of Career Group of Companies,
President Emiritus of the National Association of
Women Business Owners

How to Use
What You've
GOT
to Get
What You
WANT

MARILYN TAM

JODERE
GROUP
San Diego, California

JODERE
GROUP

P.O. Box 910147
San Diego, CA 92191-0147
800.569.1002
www.jodere.com

Copyright © 2003 by Marilyn Tam

Editorial supervision by Chad Edwards

All rights reserved. No part of this book may be reproduced by any mechanical, photographic, or electronic process, or in the form of a phonographic recording; nor may it be stored in a retrieval system, transmitted, or otherwise be copied for public or private use—other than for "fair use" as brief quotations embodied in articles and reviews—without prior written permission of the publisher.

The intent of the author is only to offer information of a general nature to help you in your quest for emotional and spiritual well-being. In the event you use any of the information in this book for yourself, which is your constitutional right, the author and the publisher assume no responsibility for your actions.

CIP data available from the Library of Congress

ISBN 1-58872-077-2

06 05 04 03   4 3 2 1
First printing, April 2003

PRINTED IN THE UNITED STATES OF AMERICA

BOOK DESIGN BY CHARLES MCSTRAVICK

THIS BOOK IS DEDICATED

IN MEMORY

TO AH YEH, TAM WING KWONG

CONTENTS

ACKNOWLEDGMENTS

THIS BOOK is the product of all my life experiences and for that I wish to thank all the people who have crossed my path, for, without them, I would not be the person I am today.

There are many special people who have contributed in their own unique ways to the creation of this book. Thank you to Kate Ludeman for suggesting that I should write a book, and to Gay Hendricks for encouraging me to start the process.

To my editor and friend Donna Beech, who can do wonders with hanging participles and can also gently suggest that I need to expand with more detail since what I thought was clear was perhaps only apparent in my mind. Thank you Donna also for your support and good cheer whenever I felt stuck; you have made the creation of this book so much more graceful and enjoyable.

To my literary agent, Bill Gladstone, who believed in me and guided me in the whole process of writing and publishing. Bill, you are a friend as well as my respected collaborator. Thank you for your support and enthusiasm.

To my publisher, Debbie Luican, what a pleasure it is to work with you and your team at Jodere Group! You have set a wonderful standard of collaboration and integrity in your company, and it is a joy to work and cocreate with you and your colleagues.

To my friends, teachers, and family who have been so supportive and patient with me even when I said I can't come out and play because I needed to write: Tom Cunningham, Jan Ingram, Owen Tam, Sophia Tam, Lailan McGrath, Amy Taylor, Audrey Thieme, Henry Chan, Andrea Rifkin, Chungliang Al Huang, Michael Petracca, Eddie Erlandson, Barbara De Angelis, Candis and Don Kjelleren, Daniel Susott, Emerald Starr, Robert Muller, Barbara Gaughen Muller, Arun and Sunnada Gandhi, Nancy Brown, Leslie Larsen, Eva and Yoel Haller, and Lily Haggerty. Thank you for your love and faith in me. I so appreciate your presence in my life.

To the memories of Po Po and my father, Tam Chak Lam. The lessons I learned from them will continue to kindle in me greater integrity, generosity, and understanding.

To Meeghus, for your love, support, and humor—what a joy it is to play, learn, and grow with you—I am thankful.

To Kwan Shih Yin, who is my inspiration for living life with compassion, love, and joy.

And to Spirit, who has given me life, guidance, and wondrous blessings. I am deeply grateful.

FOREWORD

"I WANT TO KNOW your recipe for success. How did you achieve all your accomplishments? What is your training? What was your major in college? How did you get the job?" I've had these and similar questions posed to me over the years in various business and social settings. What people really want to know is: *What is your secret for attaining business success and peace in your personal life?* This book is an answer to that question.

My personal journey shows that you can use what you have been born with to transform your life into what you want. All of us start out with advantages and disadvantages in life. In an ideal childhood, our parents help us build on our natural advantages and minimize the disadvantages we face. But all too often, the opposite occurs. In my own life, I reached adulthood at a disadvantage in many areas. Yet, I believe it was these "disadvantages" that provided me with strength and insights to create the triumphant career and joyous life I'd always dreamed of.

The key to having the life you want is inside you; you already have what it takes to get what you want. I will show you how. My own life is proof that anyone from any background can apply the Principles set forth in this book and achieve great results.

But this book is not about me. My thoughts and practices are the foundation for this book, and my experiences and background stories are woven throughout—but only as examples.

This book is for all of the intelligent, hardworking, and good-intentioned people, who work for a living, provide for their families, face real challenges, and yearn to lead a fulfilled and happy life. This book is for you.

So the question is: Can you use what you've got to get what you want?

And the answer is yes. If I can do it, you can do it.

PREFACE

IN WORK AS IN LIFE, I live by four simple Principles. These Principles keep me on course and facilitate every business and social interaction I have. They free me to be creative and productive. They enable me to see and take advantage of opportunities. They are the first things I share with my management team in every company I manage and they form the basis of our working relationship. When the team follows these practical Principles, the flow of communication is smooth; productivity and morale are high.

These four simple Principles are the most powerful, readily adoptable tools I've used in my career and in my life. I want to share them with you now.

1. TRUTH

TELL THE TRUTH ALL THE TIME. Speaking the *TRUTH* simplifies your life, gives you credibility, and opens the path to new learning and fresh possibilities.

It's less confusing. You don't have to remember what you said and to whom, and you won't trip over conflicting remarks. This one is very basic and also very hard to do at times. Often, we say what we think others want to hear to keep them happy. When the truth comes out later, *everyone* is unhappy. More importantly, there is less time to fix whatever you were afraid to say in the first place.

This has been a particularly effective tool for me, since I have a great memory—but it's very short! Telling the truth all the time keeps my mind clear of the clutter and reduces the stress of having to remember the various versions of the "truth" that have been told.

And the truth eventually comes out anyway! Remember Watergate? Enron? Telling the truth is much less painful and takes less effort. Whatever problem you're trying to avoid will be resolved much sooner if you tell the truth and deal with it immediately. Letting the skeletons multiply in the closet only makes things worse.

The reach of technology today means that sooner or later, whether it is the audiotapes or the off-the-books partnerships, the truth will win out. Deal with the issue when it appears and you'll not only sleep better, but you'll learn more quickly and insure that you keep moving up.

2. PARTNER

MAKE ME YOUR PARTNER. There are many ways you can create a *PARTNER* that supports you in your endeavors. Oftentimes, partnerships can form the network and foundation that you can leverage to achieve your goals.

If you don't talk to me, I can't help you. It's that simple. If you don't enlist your colleagues, supervisors, family, and friends in your goals, they can't support you in your mission.

In any interaction, there are always two sides: a buyer and a seller. All parties are there because they want the transaction to occur. Find the common ground and engage the others in seeing the mutual benefit. Once all parties have ownership of the outcome, they will be pulling for a positive result. From that common ground, you can all work toward the same outcome—if you make them your partner.

3. MISTAKES

MAKE BIG MISTAKES. Big mistakes usually develop into something from which you can ultimately benefit. You can make *MISTAKES* an opportunity for growth and leverage.

Small mistakes are the thoughtless things we all do when we're not paying attention. They are a waste of time and resources, and are neither instructive nor constructive.

On the other hand, big, planned, highly organized mistakes are valuable. They usually turn out to be productive in the end. Big mistakes are sometimes the result when you take calculated risks. Making big mistakes is the occasional byproduct of making big strides.

Big mistakes can only occur when you've planned and thought things through. If your carefully laid plan turns out to be a mistake, it may cost you. But it will also give you exactly the information you need to modify your strategy or change your course. You learn, adjust, and come back with a stronger, more impactful strategy that works. In the long run, big mistakes are the best feedback we ever get. The most successful people in life are those who make the best use of their mistakes.

4. SWORD

DIE BY YOUR OWN SWORD. Dying by your own *SWORD* is a metaphor for standing in your truths and holding to your convictions. It's a sure way to feel comfortable and at peace because you've done the best you can.

Fight for your ideas. If you are committed to your idea after diligent work and research, pursue it. Your supervisor may have spent an hour listening to your presentation, and you have spent three months working on it. If you're right and you give in, you'll regret it forever. Whether you do it their way or yours, you'll be held responsible anyway—so what have you got to lose? You'll have more conviction and understanding following through on what you have spent months developing than on the quick detour that your supervisor just threw in. If the project was to fail, wouldn't you rather get in trouble for something you did than for something someone else made you do?

EXAMINING THE PRINCIPLES

As you read this book, you will notice that I've notated which Principle(s) are being exemplified in each story. I invite you to check to see how these values guide every decision and choice point. I have purposefully placed the definitions and explanations to the Principles in the Preface, so you may easily refer to them. By examining the Principle notations throughout, you will see that you can choose how to regard a particular situation. In that way, you will have the power to influence the outcome. Every circumstance is a potential learning experience, which you can decide how to use to your benefit.

Many situations involve several of the Principles simultaneously. The "Action Points" within each chapter are reminders of how you can incorporate these insights into your life. To live by these guidelines requires integrity, courage, and collaboration. This is how I run my business and how I run my life. It works.

Enjoy the book. Life's a lot more fun and rewarding when you live with these Principles in mind.

WHAT YOU'VE GOT

PART ONE

CHAPTER ONE

Inside You

THE COMMON WISDOM is that in order to be a
success, you have to have certain advantages:
knowing the right people, going to the right
schools, belonging to the right clubs, looking the right
way—I am here to tell you that you can use what you've
got to get what you want.

My own life has been extraordinarily diverse. I grew
up in a traditional Chinese family in Hong Kong as the
lowest person on the totem pole: a second daughter who
was quickly followed by three sons. My childhood was
an all-too familiar litany of abuse and neglect. If the
common wisdom were true, I should have been a miser-
able failure in life, struggling to overcome a low sense of

self-esteem and fighting a losing battle to win the affection of parents who were never going to give me the acknowledgment I crave.

And yet, I managed to rise through the executive ranks of the international business world and become an influential corporate leader, speaker, consultant, author, and philanthropist.

According to the common wisdom, I didn't have the advantages you need to get to the top. Instead of having connections or running with the in-crowd, I grew up in a foreign country where English was my second language. Instead of getting an Ivy League education, I went to a state university. Instead of being one of the guys in a man's world, I'm a woman.

The lesson is this: If I can use what I've got to get what I want, you can too.

I know this isn't how the psychologists, philosophers, and rescue workers think it's supposed to be, but I believe that the struggles of my childhood—all the misery, loneliness, and grief—are responsible for my success. When I stood at the edge of my future, looking toward the uncharted terrain of my career, the skills I learned in childhood were all I had.

My life has proven that what I had was enough.

Merely surviving in my family gave me the skills and the inner knowing that guided my career and my success in life. I built on those early traits through trial and error with the help of Spirit and many teachers as I journeyed through life.

What I *did* was . . .

- **listen** and **trust** my inner voice,

- **envision** what I wanted,

- **plan** and **anticipate** the challenges,

- **learn** and **practice** the skills needed to carry out my vision,

- **confidently proceed** as the situation develops,

- **continually try** different ways to achieve my goals until I succeeded.

And what I *learned* is that what's inside each of us is powerful enough to help us achieve anything we want.

YOU'RE GOOD ENOUGH JUST AS YOU ARE

You are good enough now. You don't have to wait for anything, anyone, or any situation before you can start making a positive change in your life. You don't have to wait until you get a new job, lose 15 pounds, move to a new house, get a new relationship, an existing situation improves, or hold out for any other reason. The time and place to begin working toward your goals is here and now.

BELIEVE IN YOURSELF AND HOLD ONTO EVIDENCE THAT YOU ARE GOOD ENOUGH

Think you can, think you can't;
either way, you'll be right.

—HENRY FORD

My family was devastated when I was born. They'd already had a girl and were desperate for a boy. When my younger brother was born soon after me and two more boys followed him, I was made completely superfluous. My brothers inadvertently cemented my position as the unnecessary and bothersome child. As a result, I was alternatively ignored or punished for reasons that were mostly unrelated to anything I did.

It was a situation that had great potential for being a training ground for me to go through life as an insecure victim. If things had been different, I might have fallen into that role without realizing it. But I had a secret weapon: my grandfather, Ah Yeh. The spark of belief he had in me gave me a sense of self-worth that kept me going when others doubted me.

It was Grandfather Ah Yeh who gave me my Chinese name, Hay Lit. Hay and Lit were the names of two of the Emperors in China; one was known for his intellect and wisdom and the other for his prowess in military strategy. It was a most unusual name for a Chinese girl, but it registered with me like a permanent vote of confidence from a man I deeply admired.

I never spent much time with my grandfather. He died when I was about seven. I only saw him a few times a year when he was alive. But the powerful name he gave me made me feel he must really have believed I was strong. He must have thought I was something special.

That little kernel of hope and inspiration held me in good stead when the world around me told me otherwise. That kernel of hope and my own inner knowing always kept me going and gave me hope when I didn't know how I was going to survive the situation at hand.

You can do the same thing by holding onto any time in your life when you felt the approval or support of someone who believed in you. Dive into that feeling of acceptance. Let it sink into your bones. Cherish it as you go forth and deal with the world. You'll find your interactions much more successful when you have confidence and self-worth.

TRUST IN SOMETHING BIGGER THAN YOURSELF

Throughout time, people have searched for the meaning of life. Countless religions, philosophies, and books are dedicated to answering that perennial question: What is the meaning of life? Do we enter this world from nothing for a certain number of years and then disappear forever? Is this all there is? Is this 60, 70, 80, 90 or so years on planet earth all there is for us? What are we here to do?

I started discovering the meaning of life early in my childhood. I found that there was something more powerful than what met my eye. I found the power and comfort from a deeper source than the everyday reality. I found the power of Spirit.

As a child, I treasured my alone time, spending much of it up in the trees where people couldn't get to me. I found a sense of calm and security in the trees, which meant much more to me than just physical safety. I felt the presence of a greater power than what I could see with my eyes.

This power, which I call Spirit (and you may call God or the Universal Power), was very nourishing to me. I sensed that I was taken care of and that there was a greater plan for my life than what I could envision at that time. I felt that someone was taking care of the big picture and that if I did the best I could, I could trust that somehow the overall story would turn out good in the end.

This inner knowing gave me great comfort and courage to take steps and risks to forge ahead. This inner knowing of my connection to a greater power sustained me when the outside circumstances seemed hopeless or unbearable.

What Spirit means to you may vary from what it means to me. The key to tapping into that sense of peace and wisdom is to trust that you are part of a bigger picture. You are not just a bobbing cork in a stormy ocean. You have a reason for being on earth and you have a mission and purpose. You are unique and have a gift for the world that only you can share. As Martha Graham said:

> There is a vitality, a life force, an energy, a quickening that is translated through you into action, and because there is only one of you in all time, this expression is unique. And if you block it, it will never exist through any other medium and will be lost.

You are here for a reason. You have a unique gift to offer the world. Once you find your special talents and pursue them, whether it is to be the best carpenter, accountant, singer, mother, or nuclear physicist that you can be, you will have a sense of inner peace. You will feel that you have found your reason for being. You may have several talents and you have the choice to follow one or a combination of them. What an exciting adventure!

FOLLOW YOUR PASSION

I found my life passion and mission in fifth grade. It was my first upfront experience of the inequalities in life. I found out that the entire family of my schoolmate Rebecca lived in one rented room. It was all they could afford. Her family shared a bathroom with another family and the kitchen with two other families. I was shocked by the unfairness of life. My family lived in a comfortable house with a beautiful garden. I shared a large bedroom with my sister. Rebecca's entire family lived in a 150 square foot room. She and her siblings did their homework sitting on small wooden stools, using their bunk bed as the writing table. For them, luxury meant eating three meals a day. I was profoundly shaken by this disparity. She was no different from the rest of us, yet her home situation was so grim. Why should some people have so much wealth and others have to scrape by and survive on such meager terms?

This was no *National Geographic* magazine article or some faraway news story about nameless faces. This was someone I saw everyday and had shared experiences with, yet she lived in a world that was so different from mine.

I was inspired to make a difference in the world for people like Rebecca and her family. I was going to help other unfortunate people survive and grow from their misfortunes. I intuitively felt that everyone had value and I was going to prove it.

When I first told my family I was going to work in Africa as an anthropologist and help the Africans create a thriving society so that they could live healthier and happier lives, they ridiculed me. "What are you going to do—go over there and dig up chamber pots?" they laughed [TRUTH]. I just bit my tongue and kept pursuing my dream. Although it took longer than I had ever imagined, I did ultimately have a chance to work with the United Nations' Habitat II to create sustainable settlements around the world.

I agree with George Bernard Shaw who said:

People are always blaming their circumstances for what they are. I don't believe in circumstances. The people who get on in this world are the people who get up and look for the circumstances they want, and if they can't find them, make them.

You know what your passions are. Sometimes they are buried deep because you felt you didn't deserve to follow them or because someone you trusted told you that they weren't practical or you weren't good enough. But if you tap into your inner resources and listen to what your heart really calls for you to do, you can find ways of making it happen. You've already got what it takes. What you've got is all you need.

FOLLOW YOUR PASSION AND BE FLEXIBLE

Once you find your passion, follow it. But be alert to the feedback you are getting. Linus Torvalds, the creator of Linux, the phenomenally successful operating system, started Linux as a personal passion to improve on the existing operating systems.

But Linus was not fixated on exactly what the new system was going to be like. In fact, he offered his work free on the Internet so that others could add their input and modify what he was creating [PARTNER]. What resulted was a system, which is constantly evolving and is used by millions of people in the world. Today, Linux is still growing and developing, and Linus is a legend in the computer world.

In Torvalds' book, *Just For Fun, The Story of An Accidental Revolutionary,* he speaks about how his passion was so consuming that he didn't care about anything else. Food, sleep, and social interactions were all secondary. He worked diligently on developing the system for years and he also benefited from others' wisdom and expertise. In the end he succeeded, and in the process he also acquired fame and fortune beyond his wildest dreams.

Torvalds followed his passion but remained flexible and open. It is the best way to fulfill your dreams.

Inside You

ACTION POINTS

Hold firmly to these inside insights to get what you want:

1. You're good enough just as you are.

2. Believe in yourself and hold onto evidence that you are good enough.

3. Trust in something bigger than yourself.

4. Follow your passion.

5. Pursue your passion and be flexible.

As you can see you don't have to conform to the common wisdom to get what you want. Many successful people have achieved more with less.

CHAPTER TWO

In Your Business

BEFORE YOU CAN USE what you've got to get what you want, you have to *know* what you've got! The business world is full of people who are searching for something—the next great idea, the surefire marketing plan, the toy every kid has to have, the gadget no adult can live without. They're looking so hard for the gold at the end of the rainbow that they often don't see the diamonds glittering in their hands.

When you're so determined to get what you want, it's remarkably easy to miss the assets you already have!

THE RIGHT DEMOGRAPHIC, THE WRONG IDEA

When two friends and I developed the mission and strategy to found Wasabi, an Internet-based Business to Consumer (B2C) Company, we took a glimmer of an idea, and through a process of determining what we had, refined the concept into a bright, shiny, new company.

In September 1998, just before the peak of the B2C mania, my friends Roger and Jeremy decided to sell environmentally sound cosmetics online. Since I had spent three years working with Aveda Corporation, the largest environmentally and socially conscious beauty and healthcare company in the U.S.A., if not the world, Roger came to me for advice.

The best way to get the right answer is to ask the right questions. So I asked a lot of questions, and I discovered that what Roger and Jeremy wanted was to offer the environmentally conscious population low-cost alternatives to the existing cosmetics and healthcare products. What they had was passion, some of the skills they needed, knowledge of the relevant media, connections to potential suppliers, and possible funding sources. It was a good start.

What they didn't have was an understanding of the target market, the actual availability and pricing of products, and the potential market size. They were only missing three things, but three important ones. Without a grounding in the reality of the actual business world, the most inspired idea can fail.

After I'd carefully assessed their plan, I pointed out that Roger and Jeremy's concept had a lot of challenges in the way of its success. First and foremost was the opposition. Even today, a few large health and beauty conglomerates currently dominate the cosmetics business. Their main channels of distribution for upscale products are the department stores. Volume-price cosmetics are sold primarily in the large drug and discount store chains.

As a result, we knew it would be a struggle for Roger and Jeremy to enter such a tightly controlled market. The existing distribution channels would have tremendous incentives—and the buying power—to maintain the status quo. They would be determined to maintain their market positions and their gross margins. They would do their best to make it difficult for the cosmetic conglomerates to sell products to any upstart Internet company—much less one that was planning to discount the products.

The cosmetic conglomerates would also have little interest in selling to an unproven company that was planning to discount their products and jeopardize both their image and their profit margins.

What Roger and Jeremy did have going for them was their demographic focus. A large percentage of the U.S. population was hungry for alternatives to the existing marketplace. These people were interested in learning about how the products were made, what they were made from, and what they did to the body when they were used. And while they were at it, they wanted to get these products for a fair price.

These are the very people that scientist and researcher Paul Ray called "Cultural Creatives." According to Ray, 25 percent of the U.S. population share these common characteristics: they are well-educated, they are interested in their health as well as in environmental and social causes, they have a higher than average income, and they have an almost insatiable need for information—about what they eat, drink, wear, drive, vacation, design, and decorate. In short, they were Roger and Jeremy's ideal demographic—their target customers!

It was the best demographic imaginable. My advice to Roger and Jeremy was to ditch their idea for competing with the cosmetic monolith and find a way to meet the needs of this demographic [TRUTH]. Their redefined mission was also my life mission—to help create more harmony between people and the planet. After several more meetings and discussions, I agreed to join the team as CEO in developing our mutual dream.

Once we decided to target Cultural Creatives, we began to brainstorm. Because we wanted every aspect of the company to be a conscious twenty-first century company, we came up with the name, Wasabi—slightly exotic, hot (in taste and demand), and green (environmental). We planned for the company to have flexible work hours, telecommuting, and a host of other creative ways to maximize the value of the employees and the company.

We decided that the company would be a portal site for the Cultural Creatives—much like AOL or Yahoo—offering their own specialized Website where they could find the information, entertainment, products, services, and community that they resonated with.

We contacted companies that already served this group: the Harmony catalog, the Aveda Corporation, *Utne Reader,* as well as a host of health and fitness magazines and other organizations with compatible objectives. It was an exciting time of rapid change.

We soon found that several other groups were also planning similar concepts. We decided to develop partnerships with them so that there would be one portal with the critical mass to be the market leader. Our goal was to be that portal.

Our biggest challenge was in product fulfillment and distribution. It was reminiscent of Amazon.com when they launched and had to run down to the store to buy books to fill their orders [MISTAKES]. We learned from their experience and wanted to find the right partner to handle the distribution so that we didn't have to repeat Amazon.com's start-up pains.

I soon contacted a former business colleague who had become the president of Gaiam, the parent company of Harmony catalog. Harmony catalog had the fulfillment and distribution system for most of the products we were planning to offer. It would have been so much more efficient to partner with them instead of starting a new system ourselves. We found that Gaiam was also developing a similar concept.

In our discussions about how the two companies could collaborate, a completely new idea occurred to us. Had we been so determined to find gold at the end of the rainbow, we might not have seen the diamonds in our hands. But when we looked at what we had, we realized that we could do much more by merging the companies than by collaborating as separate companies [PARTNER]. It was a win-win situation. Jeremy and Roger would stay on as creative developers, and I would be free to move forward to another exciting new project: a new business-to-business, Internet-based, software company—Fasturn.

As you can see, what you've got ultimately determines what decisions you make and actions you take.

GREAT CUSTOMERS, UGLY PRODUCTS

There are times when you may have to look hard for what you've got because it's so well hidden behind your pride. This was the difficult lesson I had to learn in my first buying job as Hosiery, Bodywear, and Footwear Buyer for May Company Department Stores California.

I was young—eager to make my mark on the world. I took over from a buyer who was retiring after holding the position for 25 years. Freshly promoted from being the assistant buyer in the Junior Sportswear Department for young women, I thought I was trendy—and oh-so-fashion conscious. You can imagine how appalled I was when I saw what the bestselling shoes in my first buying position looked like: synthetic leather (plastic) sandals with a wedge platform rubber heel that were swift-tagged together with a piece of plastic that sold from $19.99 to $24.99. These shoes were selling so well that my department's business was growing in healthy double-digits every month. And these were also the shoes that old ladies wore as they shuffled along complaining about their bunions. I was deflated. I definitely was not relating to my products!

I had to swallow my pride and not get attached to the fact that I thought the shoes were cheap and ugly. My customers knew what they liked better than I did. My job was to figure out what it was, why they liked it, and to buy it for them. I had to look past the products that were so unappealing to me to ask what made them so desirable to my customers?

Once I asked myself: What have I got? I realized that whether I liked these shoes or not, I had a great base of business with loyal customers who frequented the department. There was a tremendous potential to build a bigger business based on my customers' needs. And with careful analysis, I could gradually update the products to reflect better fashion and quality.

This was a revelation to me. I was putting into effect what Diane, my former boss, used to say to me, "It doesn't matter what you are selling as long as it is ethical and it's what your customers want. You don't have to personally identify with it. The buying operation is the same whether you are selling fancy dresses or toilet seat covers."

I wasn't selling toilet seat covers, but I certainly wasn't selling fancy dresses either! What I was selling was what the customers wanted, and my goal was to slowly raise the taste level while maintaining the price range they were interested in paying.

Once I had accepted what I had, I soaked up all I could find out about what my customers wanted, what they liked about the products, what they considered a good value/price relationship, what other products they were interested in, how they liked to have the products presented, and how they liked to be informed.

I worked with the selling floor staff and the mail and phone teams. I spent time on the selling floor in several of our stores, discussed the issues with our vendors [PARTNER], and did market research to get a full understanding of what our customers wanted.

Finding out what I had in terms of customers and then using that information to buy and present the products to them was immensely successful. In less than a year, the department's sales and gross profits were growing in the double-digit percentages. And best of all—for my own ego— the quality and style of the products were improving while the prices were staying the same. I was delighted. And my boss was delighted as well—I was given the additional role of the lead import buyer in my product categories for all of May Department Stores Company throughout the U.S.A.

In using what I had in a loyal customer-base and then developing and delivering to them what they wanted [PARTNER], I got what I wanted: a healthy growing business with happy, loyal customers.

UPSCALE PRODUCTS, URBAN CITY BUYERS

Sometimes it is not immediately obvious what assets you really have. You may have to unravel the tangle of assets and liabilities to clearly determine what you have before you can proceed. Only upon knowing what the true situation is can you advance with confidence toward your goals.

As President of Reebok Apparel and Retail Group, I was responsible for the Ellesse division, an upscale Italian tennis, ski apparel, and footwear company. The sales of the footwear had rocketed up in the previous year, so I was especially curious when I asked myself, "What have we got [TRUTH]?"

What I found out was rather disturbing. For one thing, the hot-selling shoes had no authentic athletic function and they didn't coordinate with the clothing lines, an asset Ellesse was known for.

But the bigger problem was branding. We had an upscale brand with a prestige image and country club attitude. But the shoes were being bought by urban city teens. Our regular tennis and ski shop customers weren't buying them, but the streetwise youth considered them hip, new status shoes.

I also found that my new subordinate, the president of the division, was misusing two of the most valuable assets we had. Ellesse's strongest marketing advantages were Chris Evert, the tennis star, and her husband, Andy Mill, the U.S. Olympic downhill racer, as endorsers of the brands two key sports. The Ellesse president was using the precious time we had with Chris Evert to have her give him tennis lessons so he could improve his game—instead of using her to promote Ellesse products! He was not using Andy Mill in any marketing promotions at all, and instead was using the contracted time to enjoy social time with the couple.

Here was a tangled dilemma. What we had were products that did not reflect the brand image of stylish and elegant athletic performance tennis, ski apparel, and footwear. We were selling the products to a totally different customer-base than we planned. And we were not using what we had—two of the most distinguished star athletes to promote our products!

While there was a huge potential in catering to the urban youth market, it was a confusing and dangerous strategy for a company that was built on an upscale country club image. We could easily lose our country club customer, while trying to cater to the fickle urban youth market. Furthermore, we had no idea what the urban youth wanted [MISTAKES]. We had just happened into the latest, fleeting trend.

So, I had to make some hard decisions fast. First, I had to replace the management, and work with the new team to focus the merchandising and marketing back to the brand image. Working with our athletes we learned how to put more performance features in Ellesse's apparel and footwear. We designed coordinated footwear and apparel that were stylish, sports-performance-oriented, and had the luxurious fabrics and exquisite details that Ellesse was known for. Our new marketing campaign featured Chris Evert and Andy Mill wearing our new collection [PARTNER]. Holding our breath we forged ahead, trusting that we were doing the right thing. Although confusion existed, we were willing to take the risk to do what we believed was more strategic in the long run with this growing business.

What a great relief when our traditional customer-base—the country club, tennis, and ski customers—increased their purchases! We sold to more department stores than we ever had. And we were pleasantly surprised to find that the urban youth bought the whole coordinated look too!

To get what you want, you first have to know what you've got. Sometimes what you've got may be obscured by pride, conflicting data, or temporary circumstances. You need to ask the tough questions and be ready to deal with the good and the bad that surface when you confront the truth. The good news is that facing the truth now is always better in the long run than hiding from it. Once you know what you've got, you can go get what you want. What have *you* got?

ACTION POINTS

- Review your current situation.

- Take stock of your internal and external assets.

- Be realistic and open to the truth.

- Make sure your resources are in line with your goals.

- Strategize and utilize your strengths.

- Proceed toward your goals with focus and flexibility.

WHAT YOU WANT

PART TWO

CHAPTER THREE

FINDING YOUR MISSION

If you bring forth what is within you,
What you bring forth will save you.
If you do not bring forth what is within you,
What you do not bring forth will destroy you.

— ATTRIBUTED TO JESUS
FROM THE GNOSTIC GOSPEL OF THOMAS

MANY PEOPLE go through life working and living without knowing what's most important to them, trudging along in a life of others' expectations. They have unconsciously accepted what they have learned from family and from society as to what they should be doing. There is no consideration of whether the roles they took on are really what give them joy and inner peace. They do not look inside for the answers even when they sense something is unfulfilling about their lives. They go through life waiting for something or somebody to tell them why they exist.

Others are so busy "doing" that they do not take the time to reflect on *why* they do what they do. They do not pause to question why they don't feel joyful and fulfilled as they forge ahead, day after day. They go through their whole lives, never asking defining questions like these: "What is in me? What is my passion, my reason for being [TRUTH]?"

Without answering those questions, people will never discover the true reason for their existence. Their odds of looking back one day and wondering what it was all about are great.

YOUR LIFE: THE DASH

My dear friend, Glenn, is an Emergency Room physician and medical director. In the 30 years he's been practicing medicine, he has seen many near-death situations and many people die. It has given him an interesting perspective on our culture's attitude toward life and death. He says that we put the dates of a person's birth and death on a gravestone with only a dash in between to denote their life and contribution. For example, all we know from a gravestone inscribed with the words, *Abraham Lincoln (1809–1865),* is that Abraham Lincoln was 56 years old when he died. We do not know that he literally held the United States of America together when it might have split apart, that he freed the slaves, and that he was a powerful orator whose vision and speeches moved a nation.

The dash symbolizes our entire lives—the time we have to create meaning for our families, our communities, our countries, the world, and ourselves. We are the ones responsible for what we do with our lives. We are the ones who will one day look back and determine whether the life we lived was happy and if it was one we were proud to have lived. Like Abraham Lincoln, we do not know when our lives may end, so we need to ask the question now: "What is the purpose of our lives?" For an individual or a company, the answer to that question determines the mission. The action steps follow the mission.

Abraham Lincoln was clear about what he wanted to do with his life. He had a focused mission and he put everything he encountered through that filter. He died suddenly with no warning, but he died fulfilling his inner calling, doing what he could to achieve his life purpose.

This man was of humble farm origins, primarily self-taught, and overcame his shyness to become not only the President of the United States, but a pivotal figure in history. He brought forth what was within himself and reached a level of accomplishment that no one would have predicted based on his background. Once he found his inner calling, he worked tirelessly and enthusiastically to achieve his vision.

ACTION POINTS

To live a life that you will be proud of, you have to know your mission and follow it. In living your purpose, you will feel satisfied that your time spent on earth was worthwhile.

- **Determine what is most important for you.**

- **Structure your life in order to fulfill it.**

- **Live each day as if it were your only one.**

HOW DO YOU FIND YOUR MISSION?

When you think about that dash—the length of your life between your birth and death—what do you want it to say about you? Ask yourself what is most important instead of what is most urgent? What gives you joy and a sense of satisfaction?

These are the big questions that you need to answer in order to proceed in life. Some people find it by taking time to meditate and reflect. Other people find it after encountering some life-threatening incident. And others find it after being hit by some emotional or financial disaster. The key to finding it is to ask yourself honestly and fearlessly: What really makes you happy? What gives you inner peace [TRUTH]? Equipped with the answers to these questions, you can then organize your life to bring you peace and happiness.

I found my mission when I first experienced injustice at 11-years-old. At that age, I discovered that my friend and classmate's family was so poor that they all lived in one rented room. I was struck by the inequality of life and determined to devote my life to helping others.

From that defining incident, I discovered my life mission was to make things better—to be of service to people and to the planet. The idea of easing suffering and creating joy and peace was what gave me happiness and inner peace. From the moment I recognized my mission, I put every decision and action of significance through that screen: Does this fulfill my mission? Is there a way of doing this so that it serves the greater good?

That filter made decisions easy for me and I was comfortable knowing that whatever the outcome, I was following the right course for me. By being true to my mission in life, I was listening to my inner guide and doing what ultimately brought me peace and happiness.

YOUR LIFE MISSION IS THE NORTH POINT
IN YOUR PERSONAL COMPASS.
USE IT TO GUIDE YOU
IN YOUR LIFE DECISIONS.

*I have written my life in small sketches,
a little today, a little yesterday . . .
I look back on my life as a good day's work,
it was done and I feel satisfied with it.
I made the best out of what life offered.*

—ANNA MARY ROBERTSON,
A.K.A. GRANDMA MOSES (1860–1961)

Grandma Moses started painting in her 70s when her arthritis made it difficult for her to do her beloved needlepoint. She took up painting as another artistic outlet and was discovered by the art world when she was nearing 80 years old. She went on to enjoy her last 20-plus years as a respected and well-compensated painter.

Whether through needlepoint or painting, Grandma Moses found what gave her joy—creating beauty she could share with others. The fame and fortune she garnered was wonderful, but first of all, she had the desire and the mission to create art and share the beauty.

It was in fulfilling her inner calling and doing what gave her personal satisfaction first, not what had been prescribed by others that made her happy and successful. She used painting as a means of expressing her mission, to share the beauty she saw in her world. Painting was merely the way she expressed her mission. It was not the mission itself.

HOW YOU ACTUALLY EXPRESS YOUR MISSION MAY CHANGE WITH TIME AND CIRCUMSTANCES, BUT THE KEY IS TO STAY FOCUSED ON THE MISSION, NOT ON THE CURRENT WAY OF MANIFESTING IT.

In her own words, Grandma Moses made the best of what life had to offer. She used what she had to get what she wanted—to share her delight in the wonders of country life. First she did it with needlepoint, then, when she couldn't do that any more, she painted. She was fulfilled and contented in what she did with her life—with the dash. She lived her mission.

LOOK AT YOUR LIFE AND SEE
WHAT ASSETS AND PASSIONS YOU HAVE
AND CAPITALIZE ON THEM FIRST
FOR YOUR OWN PERSONAL FULFILLMENT.
IN THE PROCESS, YOU WILL ALSO ENRICH
THE WORLD.

When I worked as an intern in the State of Oregon Governor's office, my boss Gary was a brilliant man with several Ph.D.s to his name. One day, over a rare, leisurely lunch, he told me a story about his life that I have never forgotten. He said that when he was going to graduate school, he worked in a photography darkroom to pay his way. The work was so boring and monotonous that he used to keep his imagination engaged by counting how many photos he had to process to pay for a loaf of bread, a carton of milk, a pack of toilet paper, etc. When he wasn't doing that, he was counting the hours until his shift was over. Needless to say, he was not very good at his work.

Yet, when we worked together in the Governor's office, Gary was so engaged in his work that he paid little attention to the time. He always got to work before 7 A.M. and stayed late every night. The difference was, in that job, Gary was helping to create a closed energy system for the State of Oregon. It was a big idea that held the promise of changing the way the whole state would utilize energy. It had the potential to change the world. And Gary loved doing it. He was so passionate, in fact, that he continually motivated me to work harder and think bigger. Working with him was exciting and inspiring.

I have often thought about his story of the pure drudgery he felt in the darkroom, counting every penny he was making to survive. The contrast with his work in the Governor's office makes it so clear that you can only do great work when you're doing what's important to you. You'll never make great strides in anything you don't care about.

That's why it's so important to find out what you want. When your mission corresponds with what you really want to do, you open the doors to greatness.

Personally, I loved working in a darkroom. I fondly remember the hours I spent with my brother as a twelve-year-old, and later in college, experimenting and processing film. My brother loved it so much he became a professional photographer.

IT IS NOT THE TASK BUT
HOW WE FEEL ABOUT THE TASK
THAT MAKES IT MEANINGFUL.
KNOWING YOUR MISSION AND FOLLOWING IT
MEANS THAT YOU WILL ENJOY
WHAT YOU DO.

A BETTER MOUSETRAP

Often, people start developing a business or a project from some idea, skill, or tangible asset that they have. However, they forget to ask the most important questions: Do I believe in this? Does this resonate with who I am? Finding out *your ultimate goal and mission* [TRUTH] gives you more options for finding a way to fulfill your mission.

It is easy to be swayed away from one's mission by

what may be convenient or what seems to be obvious. I was good in math when I was in school; I was already doing college math in tenth grade. Because of the cultural stereotyping about Asians being good in the sciences, I felt I had to struggle to be clear about what I personally wanted instead of what was expected of me. My extended family and teachers were encouraging me to follow the customary science career route [MISTAKE]. But my heart was in helping people and in making a positive difference, not in working with numbers and becoming an accountant or a chemist. I had to risk their disapproval over my nonconformity [SWORD] if I intended to follow my dream of working at the World Health Organization. To be true to what was calling me, I had to do something other than what was programmed for me.

How does one know—or have the fortitude—to strike off on the path less followed? In my case, it was because from a very young age, I had to depend on myself to survive. Growing up in an unsupportive environment with scarce outside counsel, I had learned to listen to my inner guidance. I had sought help wherever I could find it, instead of waiting for someone to help me. Since I wasn't getting any mentoring or counsel from the people around me, I depended on books, nature, and Spirit to show me the way.

My childhood background taught me to ask the key questions in life. In business, it taught me to make sure that my projects were strong and viable before I embarked on them.

My father was trained as a barrister. He expected clear, incisive explanations for any of my actions. He expected me to be prepared with thorough, well-thought-out, and well-organized plans before he would allow me to proceed with any project. Whether it was a school project or a group outing, it had to be organized and explained to his satisfaction. Furthermore, since my family didn't offer any support or advice on my projects, I had to be doubly diligent to ensure I had all contingencies accounted for ahead of time. This meant asking questions and more questions so that I could minimize the risk of failure, since any failure was met with ridicule and scorn.

At every opportunity, I asked: Is this truly in line with my mission? Who is this going to serve? Is there a large enough market for this [TRUTH]? Am I prepared to do what this requires of me? What am I prepared to risk for this [SWORD]? Can I get the resources necessary to accomplish this? Can I get the support I need to do it [PARTNER]? How long is this going to take? What if it takes much longer? Who else is doing this? If no one else is doing this, why not [MISTAKE]?

Let me give you an example of how these questions functioned in a real life situation at Wasabi, a company I cofounded and sold before launching.

WASABI MISSION QUESTIONS

In September of 1998, I met with two friends to discuss developing a business to capitalize on our passion and resources to spread the social and environmental message through the burgeoning Internet business. We spent many hours and days discussing and testing concepts that might work in the developing business to consumer (B2C) market on the Internet. We decided to form the company, Wasabi, to serve our target consumer when we reached what we felt was critical mass.

These are the kinds of questions to which we subjected our idea before continuing:

Q: Why do we want to do this [TRUTH]?

WASABI: We believe in serving social and environmentally conscious consumers, and making a difference.

Q: Is there a definable market niche?

WASABI: Yes, the Cultural Creatives.

Q: Is it a big enough market to warrant our project?

WASABI: Yes, over 25 percent of the U.S. population.

Q: Is anyone else doing it?

Wasabi: In part.

Q: If it's such a good idea, why hasn't it been done before?

WASABI: The technology hasn't been invented before.

Q: Are other people thinking about doing this?

WASABI: Probably.

Q: Who are they?

WASABI: Other providers of services for Culture Creatives: *Yoga Journal, Utne Reader,* baby boomer magazines, NPR, PBS, etc.

Q: How will we compete with them?

WASABI: We need critical mass. Let's enfold them by getting them to advertise, offer products, and provide content for our portal. Let's make them part of the team [PARTNER].

Q: Do we have the financial backing to do this?

WASABI: We plan to seek funding from people we know: the founders of Earthlink, Yahoo!, major cell phone companies, Estée Lauder, entertainment people, creative writers, and other business people open to investment.

Q: What don't we have?

WASABI: Call center and Distribution.

Q: How will we get the products out to the customers?

WASABI: We don't need to recreate the wheel. We'll find an existing distributor like Gaiam's Harmony catalogue, which has an excellent call center and an extensive warehouse/distribution operation.

Q: Do we have enough of what it takes to have a high probability of success?

WASABI: Yes. Our operational people are on the way. We have pulled together the content, products, and marketing. We've gotten the financial backing and created an aggregate of providers. We're ready to go [SWORD]!

As you know from Chapter Two, Wasabi was so well put together that we didn't even *need* to launch it. We sold before we opened the doors. And our success wasn't accidental. Once the right questions were asked and answered the strength of the mission was clear.

ACTION POINTS

Ask the hard questions to make sure that your project is strong and viable before you embark on it. Here are a few to get you started, but you'll soon discover that there are many more:

1. Is this truly in line with my mission?

2. Who is this going to serve?

3. Is there a large enough customer-base?

4. Am I prepared to do what this requires of me?

5. What am I prepared to risk for this?

6. Can I get the resources necessary to accomplish this?

7. Can I get the support I need to do it?

8. How long is this going to take and what if it takes much longer?

9. Who else is doing this? If no one else is doing this, why?

US FOUNDATION MISSION

You may not always have a first time out success. I can tell you from painful personal experience that sometimes things won't quite work as you envision them. I had been determined to make a positive difference in life since childhood. And yet, I failed miserably in my first attempt at creating a nonprofit foundation that would make a difference [MISTAKE].

A mutual friend introduced me to a man we'll call Jim. Jim had a near-death experience that had transformed his life, and he too wanted to make a contribution to the world as an expression of his gratitude for being alive. With our mutual passion to give back to the world, it seemed like a natural collaboration. Since he had been introduced to me by a reputable acquaintance, who was a solid citizen in the community, I came to the meeting with an open mind.

Jim had big ideas. He wanted to create a global nonprofit that would build a dialogue between world leaders in order to foster peace and understanding through the creation of common goals for all nations. It would be a world where, as my great hero Mahatma Gandhi said, "There is enough for everyone's need, but not enough for everyone's greed."

Jim named his dream "Tolemac" (Camelot spelled backward). His vision was so inspiring that I quickly got caught up in the idea of making a difference in the lives of so many. It was easy to believe him because I had shared the same dream since childhood.

Jim wanted to fund this dream through complicated stock futures and a stock trading system. I was not at all versed in the world of investments. My life had been spent creating tangible goods and services. To me, the stock market was my father and brother's domain. I knew it was a world where vast wealth was easily gained and lost, but its machinations were vague and uninteresting to me. Because this was my first opportunity to create a nonprofit and I was inexperienced, my due diligence was completely inadequate; and in my eagerness, I totally ignored all that I learned in business about set-up and organization. Looking at Jim's lifestyle, I gathered that he had been able to make the system work and I left it at that. I took Jim at face value. If I had any doubts, I quelled them, reminding myself of how strongly his words resonated with my soul and of the fact that a reputable person had referred him.

On this flimsy analysis, I joined forces with Jim to fund and create our backward Camelot [MISTAKE]. After several months of encouraging signs, I gave him a check for a significant amount of money to support the foundation. But as time went by, Jim gradually became less and less available. Finally, he confessed that his system was not working and that most of my investment money was gone. He continued to spin more stories about how he just needed a little more time and a bit more money to make the system work.

Jim persisted on regaling me with stories of wonderful philanthropic possibilities. It was becoming more apparent that Jim's system did not work, and that my money had probably gone to supplement his family's lifestyle. Thankfully, I woke up in time to stop funding this quixotic dream. There was no way I could get my money back since it had gone into a worthless investment. Sadder and wiser, I wished him good luck, and then bade him and my money farewell. Eventually, Jim sold his huge mansion and left town.

The loss of the opportunity to realize my dream of saving the world was even more painful than the loss of a significant amount of money. When I took a hard look at what had happened, I realized that by allowing the glow of my dream to blind me, I had failed to do what I had always done in business—ask the right questions and *then* decide whether to proceed. It was a painful lesson, but one I never forgot.

After much reflection, I decided that the idea itself had been good. But the execution had floundered. I returned to my mission of creating more peace and harmony on the planet and formed a new nonprofit on a much more solid footing.

This time, I asked the hard questions [TRUTH]:

Q: Why do I want to do this?

A: I want to make a positive difference.

Q: Is there a definable market niche?

A: Yes, a large percentage of the world population is suffering from hunger and disease. They lack education and other basic human rights. The environment is degrading daily.

Q: Is it a big enough market to warrant your project?

A: Yes, I only wish it was not such a daunting and enormous market!

Q: Is anyone else doing it?

A: Yes, thankfully, and I intend to collaborate with as many as I can.

Q: If it's such a good idea, why hasn't it been done before?

A: It is being done in parts by many agencies and organizations. What I have to offer is my experience and connections to draw many of them together for greater leverage.

Q: Are other people thinking about doing this?

A: Probably.

Q: Who are they?

A: Other people and organizations that also see the synergistic power of joining forces.

Q: How will you compete with them?

A: We need critical mass. Let's enfold them by getting them to work together with us, offer ideas, and share connections to make it happen. Let's make them part of the team [PARTNER].

Q: Do you have the financial backing to do this?

A: I will start with my own funds and also work with other people and organizations that have similar missions. We plan to seek funding from people and organizations we know from other nonprofits I have worked with and from corporations, which have the desire to give back to the community.

Q: What don't you have?

A: An existing 501-c 3 nonprofit designation.

Q: How will you get one?

A: We don't have to recreate the wheel. Let's join forces with a nonprofit that is interested in sponsoring and acting as the umbrella agency for Us Foundation [PARTNER].

Q: Have you reached critical mass to have a high probability of success?

A: Yes. I have an ethical new partner who has skills that I don't. We have a diverse group of talented volunteers. We have pulled together the mission, strategy, services, and connections necessary to make it happen. We've gotten the financial backing and have a large population who is eager and in need of our services. We're ready to go [SWORD]!

Once the right questions were answered, the strength of the mission was clear. After my lesson from the Tolemac experience, I was not mesmerized by the concept only, but did the entire practical due diligence that any significant project should be subjected to. This time I was comfortable proceeding, knowing that I was doing my best and that if I failed this time, it would still be worthwhile.

The Us Foundation was founded on the premise that "There's only Us, no Them." The idea is that we are all on this planet together and we have to support each other because each person is part of the whole world. Whatever happens to one part affects everything else.

Now, seven years later, Us Foundation has touched people's lives in 12 countries. We are a member of the Partners' Initiative of United Nations' Habitat II and have helped create more understanding and harmony in people and on the planet. The work is continuing.

ACTION POINTS

1. Determine what is important for you.

2. Establish your life path in order to fulfill it.

3. Live each day as if it is your only one.

4: The mission stays the same—ways of living your mission may change.

5: Do not be swayed away from your mission by what may be convenient.

6: Make sure that the projects are strong and viable before you embark on them.

7: Proceed confidently, knowing that you are doing your best and that in itself is worthwhile.

Finding Your Mission

This is the true joy in life,
the being used for a purpose
recognized by yourself as a mighty one;
the being a force of nature instead of a feverish,
selfish little clod of ailments and grievances
complaining that the world will not
devote itself to making you happy.
I am of the opinion that my life belongs
to the whole community and as long as I live
it is my privilege to do for it whatever I can.
I want to be thoroughly used up when I die,
for the harder I work, the more I live.
I rejoice in life for its own sake.
Life is no "brief candle" to me.
It is a sort of splendid torch
which I have got hold of for the moment,
and I want to make it burn as brightly
as possible before
handing it on to future generations.

—GEORGE BERNARD SHAW
FROM *MAN AND SUPERMAN*,
DEDICATORY LETTER

CHAPTER FOUR

STAYING TRUE
TO YOUR MISSION

HOW DO YOU LIVE
YOUR MISSION?

ONE OF THE MOST COMMON CONCERNS
people have about their newly discovered life
mission is how do they incorporate it into
their lives? Do they have to completely change their lives
and/or quit their jobs and start all over again? Fear often
surfaces when a person starts reflecting on their true
calling. They worry that they may have to radically
change their lives. This fear deters many from any deep
inquiry into the purpose of their lives.

The truth is, your life purpose will make your life easier,
happier, and more fulfilling, not less so [TRUTH]. Imagine

bobbing along on the ocean currents, not having any control over whether you run into a sandy beach or drift out to the middle of the sea with nothing around for hundreds of miles. That is what life is like without a mission. As we discussed in the last chapter, your mission is the north point of your personal compass. It indicates the way and helps you navigate the ocean of life.

> *He who has a why to live for*
> *can bear almost anyhow.*
>
> —NIETZSCHE

When I am living and working in harmony with my mission, my mind chatter and second-guessing stops. Life seems to flow smoothly. Even when challenges appear, they seem to be lessons on my journey instead of barriers or warnings to turn back. I am enthusiastic about what I am doing and feel energetic and at peace.

WHO?

It hasn't always been clear to me how to live my mission. When I was younger, I thought there was only one-way to achieve my altruistic mission—by working at the World Health Organization (WHO) in Africa. All my course work and degrees in the universities were designed to prepare myself to do what I thought was my life's work. I had narrowly interpreted my mission of making a positive difference for people and the planet into a single job description. It was a total shock when I found out, upon nearing graduation from graduate school, that WHO required ten years of experience before they would hire anyone in my field.

I could have saved myself a lot of grief if I had done then what I do now as a matter of course—thoroughly research an idea before committing myself to it. An idea, regardless of its value, is not enough to pin all your hopes and plans on. You have to make sure that it is viable and that you are prepared to do what it takes to carry it through.

Waiting so long to investigate my career choice [MISTAKE] seems laughable to me now, but at the time I was completely unprepared. The news threw me into a panic. I thought that my reason for being had been destroyed. Because I had focused on only one way of achieving my mission, I felt lost and confused. Fortunately, with a few months before graduation, I had some time to reflect and ask myself the deeper questions: Why did I want to work at WHO in the first place? What did I really want?

Slowly, the answer came from inside me: I wanted to help make things better for humanity and the environment. Delving into this answer, it gradually dawned on me that I could do that wherever I was. I didn't have to go to a foreign land to help; I could help from anywhere on the planet. With that insight, I decided to interview for jobs where my skills and education could make a difference.

At my first job interview, with May Company Department Stores California, I found an industry that offered promotions and rewards based on results and merit. I was immediately interested. The possibility that I could be acknowledged for what I achieved and not judged by my age, size, gender, color, or nationality was thrilling to me. Having experienced discrimination based on all the above, this sounded like heaven. The concept of being able to do my best and be judged solely on my performance was so exciting. I could do my best work and do well by living and acting as I wanted others to.

It has always been my belief that everyone should be accepted based on who they are inside and not on their physical characteristics or other external influences. I regard each person as a good person unless they prove otherwise. Operating from the perspective that the world is a helpful and hopeful place, I find that life is much easier and less stressful than if I were a pessimist.

Meditating on my decision to accept the job offer from May Department Stores California, I felt at peace. Here was an organization whose philosophy echoed mine by recognizing, compensating, and advancing people on their actual performance without prejudice. That was my sign to take the plunge and move from Oregon to Southern California to a life that I had never imagined. In my heart I knew that wherever I found myself, there would be ways for me to live in accordance with my values [SWORD].

I had taken the leap from the belief that I could accomplish my mission with only one kind of job to the deeper, more useful understanding that I could fulfill my mission just as well in a job that was *aligned* with my values.

May Department Store had an affirmative recruitment and hiring program, and was active in social services for the community. My "mission screen" was in place to ensure that the company's mission was compatible with mine—that the company had a social conscience. I was eager to have a forum to support the expansion of that social conscience in everyday work and life.

I derived satisfaction from the fact that I would be able to impact the culture of business through my focus on integrity and service. I felt I would be able to improve and inspire others to a greater sense of social awareness and responsibility. Even though it was not the conventional way of doing good, I was convinced that every positive interaction would have a chain reaction.

As I rose in the corporate world, working in up to 120 countries, I was able to positively influence many people's lives. I didn't plant crops in the Serengeti, but I helped eliminate child labor from soccer ball manufacturing in Pakistan. I didn't dig wells in Kenya, but I helped establish manufacturing standards for apparel production worldwide. I didn't educate children in Zimbabwe, but I helped raise human rights consciousness internationally on the board of the Reebok Human Rights Foundation. In retrospect, I have made more of a constructive impact by being in business than I would have if I had been able to join WHO upon graduation.

The realization I came to was that my mission lies inside *me* [TRUTH], not in a particular job. I can follow my mission and make a difference by doing everything with integrity. I can approach each task through the lens of making the world a better place. Choosing to work with people and companies with principles and harmonious missions, I can create positive change in whatever it is that I do. Using my skills to manage and operate with social conscience, I can build businesses and societal benefit simultaneously.

My employees' morale is nourished by the affirmative company philosophy, the company's reputation and sales are enhanced by the beneficial social actions, and the community is enriched by the company's constructive involvement. In order to stay true to your mission, you have to work with what you've got.

> YOUR LIFE MISSION IS YOUR GUIDE
> TO KEEP YOU ALIGNED TO WHAT
> GIVES YOU PEACE AND JOY.
> YOUR CIRCUMSTANCES OR GOALS MAY DIFFER
> IN VARIOUS TIMES IN YOUR LIFE,
> BUT THE MISSION STAYS THE SAME.

Mimicking and mugging, I was just a game myself.
Ignorant, I thought to be was to name myself.
Full of myself, how could I know myself?
I emptied myself and became myself.

—RUMI

HOW TO ADJUST WHEN THE SITUATION CHANGES

Staying true to your mission when there is a change in circumstances can be an opportunity for you and the whole organization to take stock, reassess, and grow. It is an opportunity to question. What is the driving force behind the activities that you and/or the company feel compelled to do?

I faced this dilemma after I had been President of Reebok Apparel Products and Retail Group for about three years. At first, I noticed that something was different in the way I felt about going to work. I did not wake up energized and excited to go to the office as I had before. I had always woken up feeling: "I *get* to go to work today!" But that feeling was gone.

And the people at work seemed different, too. They were increasingly focused on divergent goals. There was less cooperation and camaraderie. People would "forget" to tell other divisions about innovative projects or developments that they were working on. More gossip and rumors seemed to be floating around the place. Soon, going to work felt more like a responsibility and duty than a privilege and reward [MISTAKE].

Listening to what my feelings were telling me, I took time to reflect on what had changed for me [TRUTH]. It had begun when a promising new market had opened up in the U.S.A. for cleated shoes—for soccer and other sports. Previously in America, cleated shoes had been primarily sold only to the people who played sports that required cleated shoes. Unlike basketball, running, and tennis shoes, there had been no interest in cleated shoes for everyday wear. And since the market was limited, Reebok had never taken an interest in developing or selling cleated shoes. European brands like Adidas and Puma had a long-established, international soccer shoe business and Reebok had never cared.

But suddenly Americans were discovering soccer. Both girls and boys were forming soccer teams. With the potential for greater sales, it was becoming an important market for Reebok to enter. But Reebok had little experience in this area. The rules and generally accepted ways of operating in this market were grayer than what we were used to. We were struggling to find a way to be competitive in a market where the road ahead was unclear and the price of entry was high. Each new shoe requires a mold, and since Reebok had not produced soccer shoes before, we would have to invest heavily into making molds for every size and each new style. It was an expensive and somewhat risky commitment since we were not yet sure how big the market was going to be. And we did not know what styles, if any at all, would sell.

The company solution was to hire someone with experience in the cleated industry. It was an obvious solution and one I concurred with—except that the final candidate for the job had a questionable reputation. Because he did not share the company's scrupulous ethical and moral standards, his purported values and actions were out of sync with the company's mission. And I was apprehensive about adding a person at such a high level who did not share the company's values. I was concerned that this new addition would dilute or even derail our culture and direction.

After much internal debate about the wisdom of hiring someone at odds with the company's philosophy, the man was hired [MISTAKE]. I felt uncomfortable with the decision. And unfortunately, it was not long before what I feared most began to happen. The company's spirit was gradually eroding. The workload was more demanding than ever and the company was doing moderately well, but there was a subtle shift in strategy and mission. Instead of working in close collaboration between divisions, an atmosphere of competition and one-up-manship began to take hold.

Because the climate was changing, personnel in other divisions were soon being hired that matched the new values that were seeping into the company ethic. These new decision-makers valued pumping up sales volume and expansion into areas where there was potential for gray, instead of clear-cut ethics. More internal obstacles and behind the scenes manipulations in the operation of company business became the norm.

Colleagues from other divisions were coming to my division inquiring about transfers. They were unhappy with the changes in their divisions and wanted to move to an area where they felt the company they believed in still existed. Less-than-complimentary rumors were coming back from the market and our manufacturers about various business and social interactions involving Reebok personnel.

My own boss was supportive, but torn. When I reiterated my concerns, he understood what I was standing for and agreed with me. However, the promise of new markets and huge new sales was even more enticing.

And it was after eight months of struggling to bring the company back into line with our original mission that I began to get up in the morning with a sense of dread. I felt stymied at not being able to effect positive changes. In fact, my insistence on pursuing the company's mission (not to mention my personal mission) was causing strife and division within the corporation.

After much reflection and meditation about what was important to me, I decided to resign so that I could continue to live my life mission [TRUTH/SWORD]. It was not an easy decision. As president of seven divisions of Reebok, I had a great position from which I was able to effect many positive changes in the company and in the community. I felt that I would be letting many people down if I left. And with the new corporate climate, I was also worried that some of the charitable work I cared so much about would not carry on without me.

But at that time, I'd been spending most of my time putting out fires instead of being able to solve problems and create added value. I had done everything I could do to change the circumstances, but it was obvious that I had to choose: either conform to the new philosophy or elect to leave. So the decision became much easier. I knew that I could only be at peace if I were following my mission.

A clear indication that you are not living your mission is the feeling that your life or work is a chore. When everything is an effort, you are no longer serving your mission. Before walking away from a job, however, make sure there is nothing you can do to realign the situation. You may have fallen into an unconscious pattern [MISTAKE]. You may be the one who is off-course. Your mission is like your personal alarm system. It can alert you to the fact that you are living in a way that is no longer meaningful.

If you have done all you can to remedy the situation and it is still unacceptable, conclude it the best you can. It is vital to learn the lessons that got you to this point, so you don't repeat them again. Then, move on with the knowledge and assurance that you have given it your all. You can go forward with confidence and feel comfortable that you are doing what is right for you.

ACTION POINTS

There are a few steps that you can follow when you feel that you are in a situation that no longer seems to be in line with your mission:

1. **Establish the reason for your malaise and discomfort.**

2. **Determine whether it is your own inertia or a correctable state of affairs.**

3. **If it is truly no longer in line with your mission, make a change.**

4. **Learn the lessons that the experience has taught you.**

5. **Realign your goals with your mission, and then move forward with confidence and grace.**

HOW TO WORK WITH WHAT YOU'VE GOT

How do you ensure that you are maximizing what you have and staying true to your mission? Such an opportunity presented itself when I joined Aveda Corporation in 1994.

When Horst Rechelbacher, the founder of Aveda, asked me to join, I had just moved to Santa Barbara, California, after resigning from my position as president of Reebok Apparel and Retail Group. I had been planning to start a nonprofit foundation in line with my life's mission.

I had known Horst for years through our mutual work on various social and environmental causes. Now he wanted to transition out of Aveda's daily operations to devote more time to environmental activism and to visionary creativity. I had known that Aveda Corporation, a beauty and healthcare company based on organic plants and flowers, had a mission that resonated with mine. It seemed to be a natural fit.

I knew that joining Aveda would mean a huge adjustment in my life, but I was intrigued with the opportunity to create bigger and speedier positive change in the world through Aveda [PARTNER] than I could from starting from scratch with my own foundation. After taking time to go inside and reflect, I put my plan to start a nonprofit foundation on hold and happily accepted the job. At that time, I believed I could fulfill my mission more powerfully by combining forces with a conscious company than by starting a nonprofit.

The first thing I had to do upon entering a new venture was to ask questions to learn the "whys and what fors." Even though I thought I knew a lot about the company, my actual participation revealed another level of depth and challenge.

Aveda had been founded by Horst almost 30 years ago on Ayurvedic principles based on the holistic use of natural resources. Ayurveda is a system of healing, which evolved in ancient India 3,000–5,000 years ago. Its philosophy and science is based on assisting nature by promoting harmony between the individual and nature, as well as by living a life in balance with nature's laws. Ayurveda promotes eating organic food, minimizing one's impact on the planet (reduce, reuse, recycle), being mindful of how one affects others, and consciously tending to the environment. Ayurvedic principles teach that living in this way can heal the mind-body complex and restore wholeness and harmony.

Because many people appreciated these principles, Aveda had developed an extremely loyal customer-base. Their customers loved and appreciated the effectiveness of its products, as well as the philosophy and conscious way in which the products were sourced, developed, delivered, and marketed. They cherished the products and supported the mission of Aveda. Customers liked the way it was sold in dedicated salons by knowledgeable beauticians who spent time explaining the company's products and mission.

When I arrived, this faithful following offered me a very strong foundation on which to build, but also a challenge. How could we expand a family style operation while still staying true to the mission that made the business successful in the first place? The company was ready for the next level of growth. How could we take it there while maintaining its character and soul? How could we increase the number of people in more locations while continuing to convey the value of this beneficial line of products?

Shortly after I began, we gathered several hundred Aveda personnel in an assembly to discuss and dream about how we might expand consciously so as to preserve and enhance the company's spirit [PARTNER]. Collectively, we took time to suggest, envision, and argue over how to remain centered in the mission, while going international in distribution and sales.

One of the most important ways of staying true to Aveda's purpose was already being done—we were being mindful in strategizing our expansion. We took the time to reflect on the possibilities and we drew up consensus plans. As a whole, we decided to make sure the company grew organically [SWORD], not by bringing in an outside team of experts to tell us how to do it the conventional way, but by cultivating our talent from within.

Several people in the company had experience in various aspects of international business, including a deep understanding of the cultures and customs of the countries we planned to expand to. Ad hoc committees of Aveda associates were formed to work on international development. Ultimately drawing on inside and outside resources, we interviewed and explored business synergies with like-minded people and companies in the target countries.

A side benefit that appeared as we worked on the international expansion was that everyone in the company started collaborating more. People from different departments worked together on various aspects of the international program. As communication and cooperation increased, so did productivity and morale.

We started business relationships in the countries where we found kindred people and business practices. It was important that we shared common missions and goals with our new partners so that our business philosophy and practices would be consistent everywhere [TRUTH].

Aveda grew rapidly and organically because we were observant of the company mission. Every step of the way, we returned to ask the key question: Is this in line with our mission? We kept our focus on our point north and had a reference as we entered new territory. After 18 months of this effort, Aveda was being distributed and sold in nine countries. As a further testimony to the success of this effort, the company's sales and gross margin grew in the double-digit percentages.

ACTION POINTS

As you try to stay true to your own mission, keep these guidelines in mind:

1. **Ground yourself in your mission. Remember to ask: What makes me want to get up in the morning?**

2. **Analyze your goals: Are they still applicable and effective in the new state of affairs? Your mission doesn't change, but the goals may shift based on new circumstances.**

3. **Involve and strategize with everyone who is a stakeholder in the outcome.**

4. **Learn and plan from the collective wisdom, while staying focused on your own reason for being.**

5. **Develop your plan, monitor the process, and fine-tune as you proceed with confidence.**

6. **Do the best you can to move continually toward your mission and you will feel at peace.**

I have learned this at least by my experiment:
that if one advances confidently
in the direction of his dreams,
and endeavors to live the life
which he has imagined,
he will meet with a success
unexpected in common hours.

—Henry David Thoreau

HOW TO GET IT

PART THREE

CHAPTER FIVE

WISDOM TO LIVE BY

H AVE YOU EVER NOTICED that some people remain calm and centered in a crisis? How do they do it? Where does their equanimity come from? Why do some people flourish in crisis while others wilt? The answer lies in how grounded and centered they are. People who are confidently living in integrity and following their mission find that details become much easier to deal with.

You may have experienced this feeling yourself when you have seen a challenge as a problem to be solved, rather than as something overwhelming or paralyzing. When you are confronting a challenge, your mind reviews and weighs different options, working through all the steps as you strategically move forward.

This is what the staff in a hospital Emergency Room does when new, unexpected crises keep pouring in all the time. Ideally, an Emergency Room staff is committed to helping and healing. They see each case—no matter how critical—as another opportunity for serving and curing. When everything is running smoothly, it is because the Emergency Room personnel remember why they are there. They are well-trained to remain calm in a crisis and alert to what needs to be done. Those who are happy with their jobs are operating in harmony with their vocation.

Their approach to emergencies is similar to the Chinese philosophy that has been embraced by many Chinese people throughout history. The idea is to see a dangerous time as a time for new opportunity and change. The Chinese words for crisis are *gna-gay,* which is a combination of the words danger and opportunity. This combination is meant to remind people that no matter how difficult the predicament may be, it is a chance to learn and make things better. Adopting this perspective can make the difference between the people who survive, and even thrive, in situations that cause others to crumble.

As a young girl in the '60s, I saw photos of the Vietnamese Buddhist monks and nuns who publicly set themselves on fire to protest the Vietnam War and their own political and religious persecution—several monks died. These public self-immolations were generally acknowledged as personal sacrifices, a statement of religious belief and philosophy [SWORD]. Buddhists have strict rules against killing in general and suicide in particular. Experts felt that these unusual actions were the expression of elite devotees who were inspired by Buddhist scriptures to demonstrate great acts of selflessness in a time of crisis.

The burnings took place with an astonishing stillness. There was no writhing or flinching. There were no cries of pain. The monks and nuns remained in meditation as they let their own bodies burn. I wondered how these monks and nuns could sit still calmly while their bodies were in flames. Their willingness to die for their beliefs and their dedication to their mission was awe-inspiring—especially when they were using such a painful and terminal way of demonstrating it.

I imagined that their convictions were so strong that they could overlook the pain and accept their own death. Or, that their beliefs were so powerful that they didn't even feel the pain and that their death was a necessary statement. It was an extreme example of how commanding living and dying in alignment with one's purpose can be. These monks and nuns were at inner peace with their mission so that the external circumstances did not shake them from their resolve. Even when it came to something as intimate as putting their bodies in a fearful, agonizing situation, they were able to retain their serenity [TRUTH].

Fortunately, most of us are never confronted with such grim circumstances. Our challenge is to be more centered in our daily lives so that we can make wise decisions and act from a place of our deepest intelligence. Participating in life from that space, you will find that everything flows more smoothly and you will be able to deal with issues that arise with calm assurance.

We create our own world by our thoughts.
And thus we make our own heaven,
our own hell.

—SWAMI MUKTANANDA

SKIING AND LIFE

The secret to being centered is to be present in the moment, neither looking back with fear to what may have happened nor looking forward in dread of what might occur.

Imagine yourself skiing down a steep icy slope that stretches your skills, and at the same time, you're allowing your thoughts to run rampant. In every unfocused moment, you face the potential of creating a clear image of falling, sliding down, or hitting a tree that would produce significant bodily harm and pain you would suffer as a result. With these thoughts sending messages of warning to your body, you start to tense your muscles. You lean back on your skis, trying to get as far from the slope as possible. You keep a furtive eye out for any other possible dangers. As your mind continues to play nonstop scenarios of skiing horrors, you are overcome with a mounting sense of fear. This kind of skiing isn't any fun. And as any experienced skier can tell you, preoccupation with these kinds of thoughts while you're on the slopes, is more dangerous than any skiing challenges you're likely to face.

The same is true in life. When things are difficult and the stakes are high, you can become so concerned about the outcome that you actually create the circumstances that bring your fears to pass. To ski down the icy slope of life in safety, means letting go of an anxiety-ridden mindset. It sounds easy but it's not. However, you do have the power to change your thoughts.

Be courageous [SWORD]. Embrace your life with enthusiasm and heart. You may be where you are by design or accident, but like it or not, it's where you are. The only way to get to the other end is to go through the terrain surrounding you.

When you approach the challenges you face with optimism and faith, your body will respond to match your attitude. It will be relaxed and alert, slightly leaning forward, adjusting automatically to the terrain. Your mind will be anticipating the next several turns, processing data gathered by your senses, and making sure you're as ready as possible for whatever you'll face next. In this relaxed, confident state, you will be able to incorporate the intuition, experience, and wisdom you have learned from others along the way. Suddenly, you will find that the conditions that were so daunting before are easier to navigate.

To thrive in life and in business, you need integrity, heart, intuition, and tenacity. Regardless of the perceived or real obstacles you face, you must maintain your focus with resolve and spirit in order to achieve your goals.

Wisdom to Live By

ACTION POINTS

To move easily and gracefully toward your mission, you must:

1. **Be calm and present.**

2. **Remember your mission.**

3. **Focus on the mission, not on the outcome.**

4. **Listen to your inner guidance.**

5. **Be open to outside wisdom.**

6. **Integrate all the information you have and act from a centered, focused place.**

7. **Learn from and enjoy the process.**

*Fame often makes
a writer vain,
but seldom makes
him proud.*

—W.H. Auden

CHAPTER SIX

IF YOU BUILD IT, THEY WON'T NECESSARILY COME

THE FIRST RULE you have to learn is one that seems negative, but is tremendously important: If you build it, they won't necessarily come.

Contrary to the movie *Field of Dreams*, where Kevin Costner's character believed that if he built a baseball field his dead father would return, in real life, you can't expect your dreams to magically be fulfilled [MISTAKE]. You have to do the research and determine that there is a demand for and feasibility to your dream before you start to build the product or services to meet the demand.

When you are enamored with an idea or are passionate about something, it's easy to assume that others are equally excited about it. But it is vital to make sure that there is a need for the product or services outside your narrow circle or perspective before you commit yourself or the company's resources to the project. If you hope to avoid unexpected and unpleasant outcomes, you must first establish what you expect in return for that particular expression of your mission, and be sure that you have the support structure to carry the project through to completion.

It is one thing to cook gourmet meals for friends and a totally different challenge to open a restaurant. You can be a much-loved singer in your barbershop quartet, but earning a living as a singer is a radically different proposition. To design products or services based on personal or anecdotal experiences without actual investigation into the viability of the concept is extremely risky. Hold onto your passion, but do your homework to make certain that your mission is a viable one.

I have learned over the course of my career how zeal, unaccompanied by enough due diligence, can cause expensive and painful mistakes. I know firsthand how easy it is to get so excited about an idea that you echo the enthusiasm of the people around you and neglect to do some key piece of research that will determine the future success or failure of the enterprise.

MAJOR LEAGUE BASEBALL

I was at Nike when I found what seemed to be active sportswear's next "big item." At that time, Nike's embroidered and highly decorated National Football League (NFL) team-themed sweatshirts were selling wildly. We could hardly keep up with the demand. While all of us at

Nike were thrilled with the performance of this item, we also knew that, like all trends, this one would soon fade. So we were diligently searching for the next item to replace it.

That's when we got the opportunity to collaborate with Major League Baseball (MLB) [PARTNER]. We were all primed to develop an MLB line of clothing quickly. Our thought was that if it worked with NFL, it should definitely work with MLB. After all, what's more American and popular than baseball?

MLB officials were delighted and eager to work with us. They were pleased with how we had positioned the athletes and given them products to enhance their own distinctive images: Michael Jordan, whose jumps were legendary, with his Air Jordan moniker and "Jump man" logo; Andre Agassi, who was known for his brash, aggressive playing style, with nontraditional denim tennis shorts; and Bo Jackson, with his football-baseball mastery, an ad campaign featuring him balancing his baseball bat on top of his football shoulder pads.

MLB officials were keenly aware of Nike's success with the NFL sweatshirt line and were eager to show that MLB could be even more popular. Researching the feasibility of the MLB project, we discussed the options with our retailers, studied the history of baseball, visited the MLB Hall of Fame in Cooperstown, NY, and immersed ourselves in the creation of what we anticipated would be an even hotter apparel line.

Everyone we spoke to was absolutely enthusiastic about the idea. It was going to be the greatest collaboration in the sports world—American's favorite sport with America's greatest sports company. What a dream team! People were already suggesting other possible collaborations: National

Basketball Association (NBA), World Wrestling Federation (WWF), and on and on. It was a time of contagious enthusiasm. Our team worked hard to develop new special fabrics, treatments, and designs to capture the baseball spirit and enhance performance. We consulted regularly with MLB officials who were equally inspired and gave us unprecedented access to their archives and ongoing moral support.

Signing a substantial contract with MLB, we ensured exclusive rights to their official logos and designs for a revenue share of the proceeds from the sale of MLB logo products. A line of MLB-themed apparel was designed, manufactured, and shipped to our retailers. With baited breath, we waited for the phones to start ringing. We were so sure that we were going to have a roaring success on our hands.

But something strange happened.

We did get calls, but they were not the ones we expected. The calls were about practical issues: How were they going to hang all the clothes in the stores? Why weren't there matching shoes with the line? What other colors or fabrics were available? And when they didn't sell as quickly as everyone expected, they called to ask if they could send them back [MISTAKE]!

We were stunned. What had gone wrong?

After drastically reducing all future commitments to the line, we went into damage control mode until we could determine where we fell short in the development process. We asked the questions we should have asked before we started. It was humbling. But it was also a great learning experience, albeit a rather expensive one. After much review, we found some clear reasons why the line didn't sell.

In our fervor, we had missed a few clues that would have saved us a lot of grief on the way to building this line. We had fallen into the trap of "groupthink." Everyone thought it was great, so it must be great. We had been so convinced that the idea was sound that we had managed to ask only those questions that would give us answers we wanted to hear. We had not factored in the differences between what had happened before and what we planned to do next. Mesmerized by our own passion, we had neglected to do what we should always do with any new project—look at it with unbiased eyes.

Despite our enthusiasm, the fact was that the line was simply too extensive for our sporting goods retailers to carry in their stores. Instead of being displayed to attract the customers' attention, the clothes were jammed into racks along with other T-shirts and sweatshirts. Customers didn't even know that a new collection of MLB clothing was available.

We had come up with a new concept, but we hadn't fully taught the retailers how to sell it. Unlike department stores, the sporting goods stores were not accustomed to presenting collections of clothing, nor did they have store space to display a collection. The marketing material we had made for the retailers wasn't even displayed by the stores. And the customers were not accustomed to looking for anything more exciting than basic active sportswear in the sporting goods stores where Nike was mainly sold. Furthermore, we had no supporting baseball footwear marketing to help sell the clothing. Since Nike made very few baseball shoes at that time, there was no baseball-marketing fund to launch an innovative new sports apparel line.

We had been excited about a great idea. And it *was* a great concept. But we didn't look ahead to the retailers and customers. We didn't bring them with us. Educating the customers about the new possibilities and providing the retailers with strong marketing support were vital ingredients in the line's success. A great idea just wasn't enough.

It was a big mistake and we learned our lesson. We sent the remainder of the stock to the retailers who did have room to display the line and gracefully got out of MLB apparel. The portion of the line that did sell had a much smaller impact than we had hoped for. Thankfully, because we had reacted quickly, we eventually did well with the MLB apparel we produced, but the line was never the blazing "big thing" we had dreamed of.

Aim for success, not perfection.
Never give up your right to be wrong,
because then you will lose the ability to learn
new things and move forward with your life.

—Dr. David M. Burns

GOOD FOR THE SHORT TERM, BAD FOR THE LONG TERM

Every now and then, you will have a great inspiration that is not aligned with your philosophy. Your product may sell, but it will not be the image or the message that you want to give to the world. When that happens, you have to decide which is more important to you—selling a product or following your mission.

Selling a product may be one of your goals. It may bring in much needed capital that helps finance the company. But if it is not in line with your mission, it's only a quick fix [MISTAKE]. And the question is, can a quick fix solve your bigger problem—being out of alignment with your mission? The truth is, any "Band-aid" solution, no matter how attractive at the time, will usually come back to haunt you in the long run.

When I was at Reebok in the early 1990s, the Reebok brand was doing well, but it was not as popular as it had been in the late 1980s. We were spending a great deal of time trying to make the brand hot again.

One spring day, one of our in-house attorneys, a bright, aggressive man, rushed into my office full of excitement. He had an idea—*a big idea*—a surefire way to juice the brand: Madonna.

"Madonna?" I said.

"Yes. She's red hot. People watch her every move. She's making fashion. If she endorses Reebok, we'll be the toast of the country."

Our marketing vice president was very enthusiastic about the idea. He had come over to Reebok from Pepsi, where he was accustomed to having music and movie celebrities promote the company's products.

On the surface, it was a good idea. Madonna was "voguing" her way across America. She had created one fashion fad after another and she was constantly reinventing herself. Around the world, women (our biggest customers) and men, followed her every move. She would be expensive, but her endorsement couldn't help but heighten our products' visibility.

But something was registering discomfort on my internal Geiger counter. I reflected on the heritage of Reebok. Reebok was a sports performance based company with the distinction of being attentive to the athletic requirements of our women customers. Reebok had grown and become successful on the basis of the philosophy that women had different needs than men in their sports shoes and clothing. We had developed and designed our shoes and clothing with that in mind. Reebok's Freestyle shoes had been the first athletic shoes designed for aerobics. It was a flexible and lightweight line of soft, leather, athletic shoes designed and sized differently for women and men. This concept had been a breakthrough in the development of athletic footwear. By responding to the different needs of the genders, Reebok had taken a risk and the customers had validated that risk with their purchases.

I was concerned that bringing in a nonsports figure to appeal to women could send the wrong message—particularly when the figure was a rock star with controversial opinions about religion and sexuality; that could cost us customers. Madonna was undoubtedly a maker of fashion. But ultimately, we were a sports company, not a fashion company. Our women customers expected performance from our products.

Gut instincts and your inner guide can set you on the right track. But you want to make sure they're supported by the facts. I told our team to do some market research to see what people thought of Madonna's suitability as a spokesperson for Reebok.

The results came in: Madonna would indeed raise the visibility of Reebok's brand and potentially increase the sales of our products. She would also send a mixed message to our customers. She would definitely sell products, but the sales would not reinforce our brand image or mission to be a sports performance company.

Having Madonna as endorser was tempting. She virtually guaranteed increased sales. But we knew what we had to do. To be true to our mission we had to be associated with celebrities who really used and understood our sports products.

So we went back to the drawing board. We asked ourselves which marketing options were most in line with our mission [TRUTH].

At the time, a dynamic, young basketball player was just coming onto the scene. People were saying he could be the next great basketball star. His name was Shaquille O'Neal. After having clarified our mission with the Madonna research, it was easy to see that this was a much more comfortable fit.

Shaquille O'Neal was an athlete identified with top performance. And he was known in a sport that was one of Reebok's strengths. But even then, we were careful to thoroughly investigate the possibility before jumping to conclusions. We did the due diligence evaluation to sign him up as a key endorser of the Reebok brand before moving forward [PARTNER].

Once we were comfortable with our findings, we signed Shaquille O'Neal as a key Reebok endorser. The rest, as they say, is history. "Shaq" quickly became one of the leading basketball players in the NBA. Selected after junior season by the Orlando Magic in the first round (first pick overall) of the 1992 NBA Draft, his stature and skill in the sport became renowned. He was selected in 1996 as one of the 50 Greatest Players in NBA history and was voted three-time NBA Finals MVP after leading the Lakers to back-to-back-to-back NBA Finals victories (2000, 2001, and 2002).

Signing an endorser who was in line with Reebok's mission paid off in important ways. As a sports player, Shaquille offered us invaluable feedback on the products from his own experience in using them. He gave us suggestions for developing new, cutting edge products and his reputation enhanced their distribution. Using his 21½ size shoes as part of Reebok's marketing display in the stores was an attention grabber and effective way of showing the functionality of our products. His exceptional performance while wearing Reeboks was a powerful endorsement of the superior quality of Reebok products. This constant validation helped market Reebok products to consumers. It is also a prime example of how potent it is to work in alignment with your mission.

In other words, establish that there is a solid knowledge base, a sound financial base, the team to make it happen, reliable distribution access, effective marketing strategies, personal credibility, and enough tenacity to get you through the first few times it fails. And with a little bit of luck you'll succeed!

If you wish success in life,
make perseverance your bosom friend,
experience your wise counselor,
caution your elder brother,
and hope your guardian genius.

—JOSEPH ADDISON

ACTION POINTS

There are a few key issues to consider before you move ahead on a project:

1. Define the idea into a functional action plan.

2. Research to establish the viability of the concept.

3. Ensure that the project is in line with your mission.

4. Proceed only if the proposal is solid.

5. Determine that there are enough resources to carry the idea through to completion.

6. Check for personal commitment to the project.

7. Check for team commitment.

8. Pray for luck.

If You Build It, They Won't Necessarily Come

CHAPTER SEVEN

IDEAS ARE GOOD, BUT EXECUTION IS EVERYTHING

GOOD IDEAS are a dime a dozen. If you've thought of it, someone else has too. But don't worry. Your idea is safe because execution is everything. And very few people have what it takes to do it right.

How many times have you seen something in the market and said to yourself, "What's the big deal? I could have done that!"

Remember Pet Rocks? How does a practically worthless piece of pebble dressed in a small cardboard box with a made up story get to be sold for $10 or $20 to millions of people? Or how about the current urban craze, push-and-kick scooters? How does a toy that was popular 50 years ago suddenly become the preferred mode of transport for children from 6 to 60? And at fancy prices, too?

It's all in the execution. For every homerun of an idea, there are untold hazards to getting it out there. The only sure way to reach your goals is to be diligent and creative in the follow-through. To reach new heights of achievement, you have to be present and mindful in the planning and implementation of the strategy.

Doing things the same old way is not going to get you anywhere except to the same old place. Having a firm commitment and passion for the idea will carry you through the times when you are weary of trying "one more time." For all you know, the next time may be the time you finally succeed.

HOW A BABY IDEA GREW

One of the first hidden gems I uncovered when I joined Reebok was a small, neglected young children's shoes division. This division had been struggling to get enough business volume to stay afloat. The management of the division were constantly under pressure to come up with enough orders to warrant production minimums. Factories didn't want to deal with them because they ordered small quantities and were always trying to get lower prices. Customers wanted inexpensive shoes because children outgrew them so quickly. Other divisions regarded them as poor cousins who were always asking for help with meeting production minimums or for design support.

Sports stores didn't like to carry the children's shoes because it was a small volume business. It was not understood nor liked by their young employees. It was not glamorous like basketball or tennis where there were celebrity athletes' endorsements and the aura of "coolness." Even the box sizes worked against the children's shoes division because the smaller boxes didn't fit the storage shelves.

Everyone agreed that there was a real need for good shoes for growing feet. Yet the children's' division team members were discouraged by the constant uphill battle they faced within the company and the marketplace.

But that was before Nancy, Vice President of Apparel Production, turned her passion and commitment to the task of uncovering the potential of the children's division.

Nancy was in her mid-30s and just had her first child. She was the quintessential baby boomer mother. Quality children's products were important to her. She and her husband wanted these products for their child and were willing to pay handsomely for them. They wanted to ensure that their child would have the best advantages to develop and grow to fulfill his potential.

But as a new mother, she was quickly finding out quality children's shoes and clothes were either hugely expensive or too high fashion for her lifestyle. There was nothing well-made, stylish, and reasonably priced for the children of baby boomers. This void in the market inspired her to devote part of her maternity leave to drafting a business plan for the creation of a new division of Reebok: *Weebok.*

Weebok was to be the brand for infants to five-year-olds. It would include shoes and apparel designed for the children of Reebok customers—people who were interested in health and fitness and who lived an active lifestyle. They had above-average incomes and wanted to dress their children in the same casual, but quality manner that they dressed themselves. But they expected to pay moderate prices, not designer prices.

Nancy was working on her business plan when I joined the company and became her boss. We made a good match [PARTNER]. I appreciated and believed in her mission. I liked the idea of providing baby boomers with a children's brand that responded to their needs and lifestyles. It was a good extension of the Reebok brand and seemed to be in line with our mission.

Other companies in the market were also realizing the need for this category of products. The Gap was opening Baby Gap Stores; Guess? was delivering Baby Guess?; Ralph Lauren was shipping Baby Polo; and many others were also responding to the perceived demand. In order to become the leader in the field, we would have to execute our plan better and more effectively than the other entrants in this budding market.

Keeping our enthusiasm in check, we analyzed our strategy to ensure that we had a viable business instead of just a pipe dream. We brainstormed on the approach and execution plan. How would we distinguish ourselves from the others? What did we have that was unique? How were we better able to serve the customers? Was there a market for what we wanted to sell? Did we have all the resources to ensure success? Most importantly of all, was the project fully in line with our company mission?

We planned every detail of the strategy like clockwork. We analyzed our existing children's shoes division. We incorporated the good and learned from the bad [MISTAKES]. Collaborating with the other divisions to leverage the company's resources, we developed a line of coordinated footwear and apparel for infants to five-year-olds.

We did field research, talked to mothers, and performed market testing. We backed it up with lab testing. We scrutinized store layouts and examined store fixtures. We shopped the competition and reviewed their advertisements. We did everything possible to make sure we were fully prepared to enter the market with a strong and consistent message.

The market was ripe for some company to become the leader. And with all the entrants, we wouldn't have time to adjust if our first line was bad. We had to take the lead and hold onto it from the start.

After we had completed our due diligence, we had to create the product. The task of developing, producing, and pricing a line that would appeal to our target market was still before us. The apparel and shoes were coordinated with each other in function, style and color. The clothing and shoes harmonized beautifully with each other and looked so cute and adorable that even those of us in the company with no children were eager to get them into production.

We still had to sell the products to the stores where our target customers shopped and to advertise so that they would anticipate our products' arrival.

After many long months of hard work and grueling travel, the line was finally shipped to the stores. In-store promotions launched the line. Our team went to key stores to train the sales personnel on the features and benefits of the products. The in-store displays and fixtures were tweaked to present the products in a consistent way. Cooperative marketing was done with the stores to create local excitement.

To our great relief and satisfaction, the customers came in to look and ... actually bought the products! And what's more, they loved Weebok! We were deluged with feedback about how delighted baby boomer parents were that someone had finally understood their needs. They told their friends about this great new line. Children's and parenting magazines called to do features on Weebok. And soon we were getting calls from other retailers to request the Weebok line.

We were cautious enough to build slowly on the success. One of the biggest dangers at this stage is expanding too fast and believing your own publicity. In the initial euphoria of positive response, you may overcommit and end up having to retrench. Having to go backwards, reducing commitments, and scaling back programs is demoralizing and disruptive to everyone involved. It also can very quickly earn you a bad reputation for being unreliable. And on top of that, overcommitment can suck up money faster than goods can be shipped out the warehouse door.

Being a new division with a limited budget, we had to allocate our financial and human resources vigilantly. So we built incrementally, stretching enough to have stock, marketing, and advertising to grow the brand quickly, but not so recklessly that we would be overwhelmed if the line didn't sell. It was a delicate balance. We scampered forward a little uncertainly, on wobbly feet, not unlike our Weebok wearers.

Meanwhile, our competition were not sleeping. They were building stores, shipping products, marketing, and advertising. We felt that there was a big enough market for more than one new children's brand, but we wanted to be at the top. As the old saying states, "durable success often comes from a lot of diligence and hard work." And we intended to be a long-lasting brand, not the instantaneous flash in the pan that's the sure sign of a fad.

After two and a half years of diligent effort, Weebok had become a $60 million business and growing. The brand was recognized and requested by customers and our repeat business was increasing as well. Other divisions inside the company were more supportive and collaborated frequently on product development with Weebok. We were building a track record in the market and manufacturers were more open to working with us; it had become easier to meet the production minimums. Other related businesses were coming to ask for us to license the Weebok name to them—a solid indication that our brand was achieving respect and positive response.

With a passionate commitment to an idea and enthusiastic tenacity, Weebok had succeeded. The idea had always been compelling, but it had demanded clarity of mission and conscientious attention in execution to make Weebok a success.

ACTION POINTS

1. Clearly state your idea.

2. Plan and review the strategy on how to implement the plan.

3. Confirm your personal commitment to the objective.

4. Solidify support for the project.

5. Check for competitive advantages.

6. Test market concept.

7. Proceed only if there is a ground swell for the product.

8. Keep innovating and be flexible.

9. Enjoy the run.

*Your future depends
on many things,
but mostly on you.*

—FRANK TYGER

CHAPTER EIGHT

You've Got to Have Passion

Ego and Willpower Alone Can't Get You There

THROUGHOUT HISTORY, there have been leaders who stood out because of the enormity of their egos as well as their accomplishments. They built successful businesses and monuments to themselves and created a cult of personality around their very being. What is usually less known about these larger-than-life figures is how much passion they had for their particular missions. Underneath the ego and willpower was, generally, a powerful drive to succeed despite all obstacles. That urge to persevere was commonly fueled by a commitment to a mission. Contrary to what many people believe, the success these leaders achieved was not due to the size of their egos, but to their passion and dedication to their vision. It was this strong devotion to a cause that drew people to their leadership.

That is not to say that some legendary leaders haven't had enormous egos. Although an overbearing ego can be off-putting and destructive when it blinds people to reality and the common good, ego strength helps a leader persevere in the face of obstacles that would have caused people with less confidence in themselves to quit long before. A strong ego and willpower can be good supports to the central core of steadfastness to a purpose. If you acknowledge the danger of having pride obscure your perspective, you can use your positive self-esteem to energize you in reaching your goals. When you are aware of the balance between being egotistical, having self-respect, and aspiration, you use that power to enormous advantage.

Without a deep core passion to anchor your efforts, it will be tough to stay the course when adversity and disappointments rain down. If the goal is significant, it is inevitable that unforeseen mishaps and emergencies will appear along the way. When the scope and demands of a project are extensive, you can't possibly anticipate all contingencies. These challenges test your allegiance to your goal. By having a deep dedication to your mission, you will keep going when others have given up.

Nothing great in the world
has ever been accomplished
without passion.

—G.W. F. HEGEL

FROM A KITCHEN SINK TO HOMES AROUND THE WORLD

One hot afternoon during an Aveda company retreat at the Aveda Spa in Osceola, Wisconsin, Horst Rechelbacher told the story of how he had started this world-class company. It was a true story of how a leader committed to a mission overcame incredible barriers to his dream.

Horst grew up in a family of moderate means in Austria. He was an indifferent student and, by age 14, he was shunted off into a trade school by the education system. The trade he learned was hairdressing, for which, thankfully, it turned out he had a natural talent. In just a few years, he became very well-known. Before long he was jetting around the world to style celebrities' tresses. He lived the fast life, traveling widely and creating a cult following. His life was glamorous and the names of his clients read like a list of the rich and famous.

Then fate intervened. When Horst was in Minnesota doing a fashion show one year, he was badly hurt in a traffic accident. After an extended stay to recuperate from his serious injuries, he was confronted with another challenge. Not having medical insurance in the United States, he had to stay in Minnesota and work to pay off his medical bills. He ended up liking the place so much that he decided to settle there.

Soon he resumed his jet-setting lifestyle, partying as hard as he was working. And again, fate intervened. Burning his candle at both ends [MISTAKE] caught up with him, and this time, he became extremely ill. Western medicine seemed to have no cure for him. Only with the support of his mother's herbal ministrations did he slowly and painfully recover his physical health. But his mind was still tormented.

The illness had made him ask the big questions: What is the meaning to my life? What am I here for [TRUTH]? Like many before him, he journeyed to India to seek answers. The time he spent there in deep meditation with Indian sages gave him clarity of purpose. It was in India that Horst found his mission: to use the Ayurvedic principles (mentioned in Chapter 4), the holistic use of natural resources, to help better the world. Those principles promote eating organic food in order to minimize the impact on the planet, to heal the mind-body complex, and restore wholeness and harmony.

Horst was inspired to incorporate Ayurvedic philosophy into both his personal life and his work at his hair salon [PARTNER]. It was a tremendous internal shift from his high-flying former life. With his life mission, he was grounded in a deeper place and felt more inner peace. He started creating healing potions in his salon and in his kitchen, combining the wisdom and knowledge he had learned from his herbalist mother and from the principles of Ayurveda.

His first product was not exactly a glamorous item—it was a bowel cleanser. It did not receive a single positive response from his clients. He went back to the kitchen sink. How was he going to share his enthusiasm and belief in the efficacy of healing and nurturing powers of the Ayurvedic system if he couldn't get his clients to listen?

Not deterred by his initial dismal failure, he kept experimenting. His firm conviction in the truth of his mission strengthened his resolve in spite of the apparent lack of interest in his products. He developed various potions and concoctions. Giving them to his clients to sample, he offered impassioned explanations of why they were so beneficial. Again and again, he got negative feedback: "It's not for me . . . I don't want to try an untested product . . . I like what I am using . . . Thanks, but no thanks . . . I'm fine . . . I don't want to change anything . . ." and on and on. A person with lesser commitment to a mission would have given up. After all, he had a good business, why rock the boat?

Horst persisted in following his mission. After seemingly endless trials and rejections, he finally hit upon something that his clients were interested in trying: Shampure, a nurturing shampoo for different hair types. His clients loved it.

Gradually, the line of products grew. Now Horst enhanced his fame as a hairstyling master with fame as a hair care genius. His zeal and fervor in spreading his mission caught the imagination of other salon owners and their clients. Customers were telling their friends about the great products, which were good not only for their hair, but also were good for their bodies and the environment. Salon owners converted their salons into Aveda products salons all over the country.

Aveda Corporation, the Ayurvedic inspired name he gave his company, was becoming a well-known brand. He enlisted and encouraged others to join in his mission, to help, heal, and beautify the world by living under Ayurvedic principles. Other hairstylists came to learn from him. An Aveda health and beauty school was established in Minneapolis to train people in the vocation. In his personal appearances at hair shows and salons, he was treated like a media celebrity. Soon, there were Aveda salons in most every state.

Today, Horst is a legend in the health and beauty business and stories about his creativity and his exploits abound. A huge myth of personality has grown up around him. Wise sayings and witticisms are attributed to him—whether he actually said them or not. I heard about his likes and dislikes from people in the business long before I even met him. Rumor had it that Horst could detect any synthetic scents and was very offended by them. Before our first meeting, I took extra care with my grooming to be sure I was scent-free. I had the impression that he would be a much larger than life figure. He did not disappoint.

Over the years, Horst's innovative holistic approach to the health and beauty business has inspired many others. For most of the people in his industry, he is known as the eccentric, demanding icon of the health and environmental movement. All they see is a legendary character clad in avant-garde clothing, speaking in the accent of his native Austria. He is colorful enough to rise easily to the challenge of becoming the stuff that myths are made from.

Stories of his ego, willpower, and temper float about. But most people do not know that the true driving force in the realization of his dreams was his dedication to his mission. Without a deep-seated passion, Horst would not have had the endurance to keep going through failure after failure [TRUTH/SWORD].

Ego and willpower will take a person so far, but they can be hard and joyless taskmasters. By itself, no goal is compelling. No matter how good the idea, no one will go through the inevitable—and often painful—ups and downs of making it happen unless they really care. Those who reach their goals must have a passion driving them, a personal fervor. When you are following your mission, the setbacks become lessons to be learned in order to do better next time. The joy and desire to be doing what calls to you will make the journey much easier to travel. It's simpler, more effective, and certainly more satisfying to find your passion and follow it.

ACTION POINTS

1. Stay true to your mission.

2. Acknowledge your healthy ego and ambition.

3. Align with others who share your mission.

4. Leverage your collective energy and zeal to achieve your common goal.

5. Take comfort in your dedication when the unexpected happens.

6. Celebrate each day and each small accomplishment.

7. Remember to share the glory.

You've Got to Have Passion

*Adventure isn't hanging on a rope
on the side of a mountain.
Adventure is an attitude that we must apply
to the day-to-day obstacles of life—
facing new challenges, seizing new opportunities,
testing our resources against the unknown,
and in the process discovering
our own unique potential.*

—John Amatt,
organizer and participant in
Canada's first successful expedition
to the summit of Mt. Everest

CHAPTER NINE

CHARISMA IS ESSENTIAL, HAVE IT OR HIRE IT

C HARISMA IS THE DIFFERENCE between a good idea and an exciting idea, between reliable sales figures and skyrocketing sales, between polite applause and cheering crowds. Wherever there's incredible success, there's charisma. You can't get by without it. If you have it yourself, great. If you don't, find someone who does and pay him or her well [PARTNER]— they're worth it.

You may not be able to define it, but charisma is like talent: You know it when you see it. It's the magic that makes people believe, the difference between making a hard sell, and having people clamoring to buy your products. When you're in the presence of someone who has it, you just know it. They may not have impressed you right away, but once they start talking, something happens. You get caught up in what they're saying. Without even noticing at first, your eyes light up like theirs, your heart beats just a little faster, and you're sitting on the edge of your seat.

We usually associate charisma with people. But a brand name can have charisma too. It can give a product a cachet that makes it "hot." The same product without the name just doesn't seem as appealing. Think of the brand names you reach for automatically. The biggest ones have become so ubiquitous that they've become a generic name for the products themselves—Kleenex, Xerox, Styrofoam, and Levi's. Do you reach for the Kleenex brand because it's better than the other tissues or because the name elicits a certain cachet? A brand name with charisma attracts people above and beyond a simple need.

CHARISMA MAKES A NEED A WANT

I don't mean to slight the necessity of proper preparation and good follow through, but the presence of charisma sure speeds the process along! It's a fact of life that any time there are two competing bids in business, the winning bid is won, more often than not, on the personal charisma of the presenter.

You have to have charisma in any entrepreneurial team or business. It's critical in any enterprise where there is a high degree of uncertainty and risk. Ultimately, people have to sell the ideas and the project, and close the deal. Investors have to have faith in the people selling the plan. Charisma is the ingredient, which helps us differentiate between countless choices.

All entrepreneurs need charisma. That makes people believe them. You've got to have something to get people jazzed about what you're doing. If you don't have it, either work on developing it or get someone who has it. It's critical.

Even in a time when everything is reduced to the bottom line, success relies on presentation. Nothing is ever sold by paper alone. It's the people. You have to have people leading the way who have charisma and drive. You need the magic.

Keep in mind that what people are buying is really the pitch—and the product. Nike and Reebok make indisputably excellent shoes. But the sales figures go through the roof on the mystique of the marketing. It's not purely about exposure to a certain number of households. It's the effect of charisma [PARTNER].

GETTING CHARISMA

How do we recognize charisma? It looks different in different people. It's not a physical characteristic they have. It's something you feel when you are with them. In products, it's something embedded right in the product that makes you feel good about yourself when you are wearing or using the product. It is elusive, but unmistakable.

How do you know if you have it? If you wonder, you probably don't have it. If you can get your point across and persuade people to follow your lead easily, you have it. When you walk into a room and people seem to just light up and listen intently to what you have to say, you have it. When things that you say are taken as truth with little question, you have it. When you've been voted most popular person in your school or organization, you have it. When it's easy for you to get better service or special treatment at restaurants, hotels, and airports, you have it. This charisma is powerful stuff!

The obvious question is: How do you get it? Or, how do you get more of it? Charisma is like a magic trick. When you break down the components, it's not so mysterious.

The most important part of charisma is your own belief in yourself and your products. Your personal conviction in yourself and your products is transmitted in everything you say or do; it fills your very being. A genuine confidence in the rightness of your purpose conveys to others a solidity and groundedness that they will feel comfortable aligning with.

In all the famous leaders in history, their personal resoluteness to the cause that they are advocating is what makes them so credible. One of the most famous of American declarations,"Give me liberty or give me death," was spoken in a speech given by Patrick Henry on March 23, 1775. Patrick Henry's passion, communicated so eloquently, helped to spur the leaders of the American colonies to move toward secession from Britain [TRUTH/SWORD]. The strength of his commitment to freedom from what he regarded as bondage to British rule made him a very persuasive personality. Others were drawn to his perspective from the deep conviction he exuded. His speech came from a heartfelt place. The words carried such honesty and fervor that they touch us even today as we read it:

> *This is no time for ceremony. The question before the House is one of aweful moment to this country. For my own part, I consider it as nothing less than a question of freedom or slavery; and in proportion to the magnitude of the subject ought to be the freedom of the debate. It is only in this way that we can hope to arrive at truth, and fulfill the great responsibility, which we hold to God and our country. Should I keep back my opinions at such a time, through fear of giving offense, I should consider myself as guilty of treason towards my country, and of an act of disloyalty toward the Majesty of Heaven, which I revere above all earthly kings . . .*
>
> *Why stand we here idle? What is it that gentlemen wish? What would they have? Is life so dear, or peace so sweet, as to be purchased at the price of chains and slavery? Forbid it, Almighty God! I know not what course others may take; but as for me, give me liberty or give me death!*

Patrick Henry's passion oozes right from the page as you read his words. It is that conviction of purpose that moves people and attracts followers. Usually the issues we are dealing with are not as significant as what he was dealing with. Our intentions may simply be to have a graceful, easy flow in our work and in our lives. Having charisma can inspire thousands of pioneers to forge a new nation that will change the history of the world. It can make the difference between success and failure of entrepreneurial opportunities. Or it can simply help smooth out the rough spots that appear in daily life.

THROUGH SNOW,
TRAFFIC, AND PARADES

*Sales are contingent
upon the attitude of the salesman—
not the attitude of the prospect.*

—W. Clement Stone

The funding of Fasturn, one of the companies I was involved in, is a good example of charisma-in-action.

Frank Litvack, M.D., a renowned cardiologist and successful medical entrepreneur started Fasturn. In 1998, he was inspired to start a medical and pharmaceutical supply company online. As he researched the field, he found that entrepreneurs who had preceded him already swamped the field.

But he knew there would be other companies that could benefit from the streamlining and efficiency that an online sourcing and purchasing system could offer. After doing his research and weighing his options, he decided on the apparel industry.

The apparel industry is a traditional and old business, which has barely changed in the last 50 years. It is still conducted mostly by face-to-face meetings and back and forth negotiations about clarifications and modifications of the production specifications and prices. Much time and money is expended to do things that could be easily done by a computerized system of standardized communication and negotiation modules.

Frank recognized all of this. His research had also revealed that the apparel industry was suffering from shrinking profit margins. Frank reasoned that this increased pressure would drive the companies to find fresh ways of cutting costs. This industry seemed poised to adopt a new way of doing business.

With the enthusiasm of a new convert, Frank put together a business plan and started the process of developing a new business devoted to serving the apparel industry's software needs. His enthusiasm and personal charisma in explaining his dream was such that he was able to recruit senior executives from JC Penny, Oxford Industries, and Bankers Trust, among others, to join him in his quest. Here was a man who had no background in the apparel business and no prior exposure to this complex and relationship-based business, yet he was able to recruit respected professionals to join him in this apparel service business, whose concept was still unclear.

A mutual friend, who was a former senior executive with Salomon Brothers, had already bought into the dream and joined him. She introduced me to Frank. After consulting with Frank for a few months in the development of the business strategy, I was persuaded to join Fasturn as President. He painted a picture of how, together, we could make a difference in revolutionizing the apparel industry.

Using the full force of his charisma, Frank projected that Fasturn would help level the playing field for small and medium size brands and companies around the world. Companies that had not been able to take advantage of international markets and manufacturing facilities would now be able to do so with Fasturn's new Web-based software. They would be able to locate resources and communicate with suppliers all over the world. As prices and communication improved, these companies would benefit from the expanded reach and detailed records in a way that would enhance their sales and gross margins. Consumers would be able to get the clothes that they wanted more quickly and at better prices. It would be a win-win situation for everyone. All we had to do was raise the money, refine the business plan, and build the organization and the software.

Frank's charisma gave him the ability to weave the bigger picture to engage everyone's interests. Using it, he was able to sell people on the promise of the company's mission—on the possibility of what could be. He was so successful at enlisting others into his vision that many people left other more certain career paths to join him. I was one of them.

Needing to raise more funds to take the company to the next level of development, Frank and I went on the road. On one particularly hectic day, we had presentations scheduled with investment companies in both New York City and Boston. Our first presentation in NYC was a roaring success—so much so that we were running a half hour late for our next appointment. (And we still had the presentation in Boston.) Traffic was heavy, it began to snow, and then the St. Patrick's Day parade started, blocking the streets of New York and all the traffic to a complete standstill.

Abandoning hope that we could do both presentations together, we decided that we would each take a presentation. I would do the one in New York and Frank would head straight to the airport to try to get to Boston before the snow really came down hard.

By the time I arrived at the meeting with the venture capitalists, I was an hour late. My hair was wet from the snow and slush. My shoes were soggy. As I came traipsing in, the receptionist told me, with a chill in her voice, that I would have to wait. The implication was clear: Venture capitalists are not used to being kept waiting.

Although we had called ahead to notify them that we would be late and they had agreed to meet us when we arrived, they were now busy with other, more important issues. They would talk to me at their convenience.

Despite my awareness that the meeting was off to a bad start because of the delay, I was relieved to have the time to catch my breath after running through the St. Patrick's Day crowds in the slushy snow. While I waited, I composed myself and turned to my briefcase to get my material ready for the meeting. But it was gone. I suddenly realized that the CD with the Power Point presentation that showed Fasturn's software functions was with Frank on the plane to Boston.

Quickly reviewing my options at this point, I realized my only hope was to be honest, to ask for their indulgence, and do the best job I could with virtually no support material.

When the venture capitalists finally invited me to join them in their conference room, they told me I would only have 30 minutes, instead of the hour we had originally scheduled. But I was ready. I apologized again for my delay, explaining about the traffic, the snow, and the parade, which had caused not only my tardiness but also the absence of Frank, whom they had expected to be at the meeting. Thanking them for their flexibility, I promised to be concise as I explained why a partnership would be beneficial for both parties.

Smiling and confident, I launched into a glowing overview of why they needed to have Fasturn in their portfolio of companies. Since I truly believed in our company and our mission, it was easy to tell the story—with or without Power Point. I described how our products would benefit the apparel industry and how they would be an integral part of the revitalization of the apparel industry. It was obvious to me that our products would be widely adopted by the whole industry and I told them so. I explained to them that it made good business sense for them to invest with us, since we were a winning team that was out to do good and revolutionize the industry. I showed them how their need to invest wisely and profitably would be met by funding the development and growth of Fasturn.

My goal was to make *their need a want* to invest in Fasturn. After an hour and 20 minutes, with many questions and animated interruptions, I walked out with a verbal commitment for a $5 million investment—this from a meeting where I'd arrived soaking wet, an hour late, and without my materials.

What had happened? How had I turned a potential disaster into a substantial financial investment and endorsement in our company?

It worked because I practiced what I knew to be the key aspects of charisma:

- I was present.

- I was honest.

- I was committed.

- I believed in what I was doing.

- I listened.

- I responded to their concerns.

- I made *their need a want* for my product.

- I was lucky.

- I was blessed.

*Luck happens when opportunity
encounters the prepared mind.*

—DENIS WAITLEY

ACTION POINTS

1. Ensure that you are living in line with your mission.

2. Establish whether or not you have charisma.

3. Evaluate the personal characteristics that are most effective in presentations.

4. Learn what works for you.

5. Be mindful and present in every situation.

6. Pay attention to what other people want.

7. Speak from your heart.

CHARISMA IN A LABEL

A company can have charisma. In fact, most companies that experience long-term success do.

In the mid-1980s, I was the divisional merchandise manager of women's wear at the Miller's Outpost Stores. Miller's Outpost had over 320 stores in the western U.S.A.

catering primarily to young men and women's clothing needs. They had built their business on the sale of jeans and, over the years, had become known for the best jeans selection. Guess? Jeans were just coming onto the market and they were hot. Some of our stores could not keep them in stock; they would sell out within a few days of arrival, even though they were expensive compared to other brands, costing over $40–$50 a pair when many other jeans sold for half the price.

Guess? Jeans were so popular because they had successfully marketed the premise that they made a wearer look shapelier and more attractive than any other jeans. They also aligned themselves with coolness. According to an ad campaign that was ubiquitous on billboards, radio, and print, you were cool if you wore Guess?. They spread that same message in everything they did: in their advertising, promotional material, the models they used, and even the production facilities they used overseas. I even saw Guess? marketing posters extolling the great Guess? look in the factories in Asia where they were made!

The hottest style was one called the "Marilyn" jean named after Marilyn Monroe. It was worn skintight and was so fitted that, without the zippers on the ankles, no one would've been able to pull them up. Whenever we received a shipment they would zoom out the door. We could not get enough supply to keep them in stock.

Since Miller's Outpost had their own private-label jean program, my buyers and I were eager to understand the success of Guess? Jeans. What made them so hot? What was unique about their fit? Was there something special about the fabrics, cutting patterns, zippers, colors, or the styling? We tried the jeans on fitting models and on ourselves. We measured them, wore them out, washed them, and tried all over again. We asked ourselves, in vain, whether it could be some synergistic combination of all the factors, rather than any individual element. But we could not find anything revolutionary about them. Everything Guess? Jeans had, their competitors had to some degree as well. (Of course, that didn't stop us from buying several pairs ourselves! We didn't want to miss out on looking shapelier and more attractive—just in case there was anything to it!)

Then one day something gave us a clue into the magic of these jeans.

It had something to do with the charisma of the label and the brand. The fit and the jean itself became almost secondary in the customers' minds; they were interested in identifying with the label and brand first. Since Guess? Jeans were in so much demand and were more expensive than other jeans, the theft rate on them was very high. To reduce theft, we had taken measures to keep them further away from the door and to add a security tag to each jean. After we moved the jeans, we noticed gradually that the stock was not selling as fast as it had been before. Instead of selling out of our order in about two weeks, we would still have stock at the end of the month when our new shipment came in.

Taking a closer look at the stock and surveying the sales people and customers to determine the problem, we found an interesting twist. Because the jeans were harder to steal, people were bringing razor blades into the store and cutting the Guess? label off, then stitching it onto their jeans at home so they would look like Guess?.

That's when we realized the popular demand of Guess? products was largely due to the brand's charisma. Their phenomenally successful positioning and advertising campaign was the key ingredient in their success. The brand's image was so strong that the label alone soothed part of the customer's desire to look good and feel cool. You could appear "cool" and "with it" by wearing a Guess? label, even if you'd stitched it onto a pair of generic jeans yourself. And it was certainly cheaper to just stitch the label on than to spend $50 for a new pair of jeans!

As even further proof that it was the power of the brand name and not the jeans, no one would buy the Guess? Jeans once the label had been cut off. The fit, fabric, and the cut meant nothing without the label.

Remember, snake oil sells because of the magic that's *not* in the bottle. What people are buying is really the brand, salesperson, image, and promise—not so much what's in the bottle. It's about the chance to buy into magic.

ACTION POINTS

To give a company charisma, you have to:

1. **Define your company mission.**

2. **Strategize and follow through on your mission.**

3. **Find a consumer *need* in line with your mission and make it a *want*.**

4. **Consistently project the same message.**

5. **Pray for luck!**

CHAPTER TEN

ASK THE RIGHT QUESTIONS

And Ask Them Now, Not Later

ASK QUESTIONS, get answers; it seems simple but it's often not. Frequently, we don't ask enough questions or the right questions.

There can be a number of reasons for that—we may think we already know the answers, we don't want to offend the others by asking, or we are just not mindful enough to think of the questions that should be asked. Only later, to our regret, do we find out that we should have probed more deeply before making our decisions [MISTAKE]. The questions we didn't ask would have given us information, helped us modify our strategy, and made a positive difference in the outcome.

Making such a mistake can be invaluable if you apply the lesson you've learned. But all too often, people forget the lesson of the past. The next time they're in a similar situation, they make the same assumptions that they know all they need to know and neglect to ask the important questions again. So, the pattern continues.

SAME PEOPLE, DIFFERENT ANSWERS

Assumptions are dangerous. The old saying, "to *assume* is to make an *ass* out of *u* and *me*," has enough validity to bear repeating. A funny story about the dangers of assumption and not asking questions comes from one of my first jobs with significant responsibility. It is a lesson that I remind myself of regularly, so I don't repeat it.

In 1980, when I became the new merchandise manager of all international divisions of Britannia Sportswear, I promoted my former assistant Olivia to my former position as director of design and development.

We were based in Hong Kong, the international production and design development center for Britannia, which was headquartered in the U.S.A. Britannia Sportswear was the premier jeans company and at the cutting edge of the young men's and women's casual wear market. It was an exciting time.

The company had pioneered the denim patchwork jean, which put the company on the fashion map. All the young and wanna-be young in the U.S.A, as well as Europe, wore Britannia jeans. Our new jeans with embroidered back-pockets, our rayon Hawaiian-print shirts, and our lines of casual sportswear had created a wave of popularity. We didn't mind working the long crazy hours because it was fun to be involved in the whole process from the first concept all the way through the finished products.

Olivia was a real whiz at design and development. She could get things done that lesser people would have said was impossible. The designers in the different divisions constantly wanted changes to their designs, fabrics, or to change the colors they submitted—and they wanted them fast. Olivia knew all the dye houses, all the sample factories, all the piece goods sources, all the knitters, and all the accessories manufacturers—practically everyone in the apparel business in Asia. She could call up any of them and have them rush something to us or to move things ahead for us [PARTNER].

Our group worked closely together to make sure that the designs and fabrics were translated into what all the Britannia divisions around the world had in mind when they cut the swatches, pulled the color chips, or sketched the pictures. It was an efficient team. Being located on various parts of the globe, the different divisions collaborated as well as we could have hoped for.

I believed it would be a natural and easy transition for Olivia to head the Design and Development Department when I moved up. After all, she knew more about it than almost anybody else in the business. But once she got into the position, something went wrong.

I started getting complaints about Olivia's management, and the president of the company did too! The colors weren't right, the swatches didn't match, the samples didn't look correct, the measurements were off, and everything was late. Olivia started working harder and her whole team stayed even later. It seemed like they never went home—staying past midnight every night, coming back early the next morning. But the complaints kept coming in.

I tried to help as much as I could, considering my new huge workload and heavy travel schedule. But my efforts seemed to be only useful in the cases that I worked on; it did not help her overall department. Finally, in frustration, with the various divisions begging me to do something, I asked Olivia if she would mind if I spent a few days with her and her team so I could watch the department in action.

Understanding the sensitivity of my coming back into my old territory, and not wanting to supplant her authority, I tried to keep a low profile. But as I watched, I started asking questions—lots of questions: How do you prioritize the requests from the different divisions? How do you prioritize within each division? How often do you communicate with the various designers? What about the countries' merchandisers? How do you update them on the status of their requests? What about the sample status reports? And the color fastness test results? And the tensile strength and other fabric tests? Which, of all your requests, are the most critical? The new sample requests show different measurements than the last one, which one is right?

They were simple questions about things they were doing, or should have been doing, everyday—things that I did everyday when I was in Olivia's position.

And as the questions did their work, the problem became clearer and clearer. I soon found myself thinking of that classic phrase from *Cool Hand Luke,* "What we've got here is failure to communicate."

Olivia and her team had been so eager to prove that they could do the job that they had dived headfirst into the work. However, they didn't ask many critical questions

[MISTAKE]. So naturally, they didn't have the answers they needed to provide the information I had always supplied to the designers and country merchandisers. Olivia and her team had just assumed that the designers and merchandisers would know that they were working as hard as they could to get them everything on time—and that hard work would be enough.

I was mystified. Olivia had been with me when I was doing her job. She'd seen me prepare the updates and listened to me ask the questions I had regularly posed to the designers and merchandisers. In fact, she'd helped me with many of them! Yet, for some reason, when she took over the department, she didn't take on the duties I performed. Since the company was young, no detailed job description existed. I had improvised and created the job myself, adjusting the job description to match the new challenges that were constantly coming my way. Olivia was having a difficult time adapting to this method of operation.

She continued to do what she had done well before—working with the fabric developers, the lab, and the design and development support team in Hong Kong—but she didn't rise to the new position. And she didn't ask for help.

As could be expected with a new director, the designers and merchandisers were leery. They weren't sure that she knew their markets. But like Olivia, they didn't ask questions. They just assumed she didn't know and let their unfounded judgment view everything Olivia and her department did with skepticism.

Ironically, the solution to the problem of no one asking enough questions was—you guessed it—to ask more questions. In order to unravel the miscommunications and judgments on both sides, we had to ask a lot of questions [TRUTH]. The questions helped redefine expectations and responsibilities on both sides.

Olivia and I asked each division and each department for a list of priorities. We asked how they wanted to receive communications—by phone, fax, telex, overnight mail, and/or in person—and how frequently? We looked for ways in which each side could make the relationship better. We wanted to know what they had learned from the past challenges. Did they really know who the other party was? We used the whole episode to improve and streamline the operation. It became a fun bonding experience that drew the various departments and divisions together much more than before [PARTNER].

The most telling incident occurred with a Canadian merchandiser we'll call Jack. Of all the merchandisers, Jack had been one of the most critical of Olivia and her team. Olivia and I wanted to especially make sure that he was comfortable with the communication and processes we were putting in place. When we asked him for his response, we learned that Jack felt somewhat mollified, but still had concerns about Olivia's team. He didn't feel that they had the capability of doing a good job matching the fabric colors to the sample color chips his team required each season. We agreed that we would be especially vigilant and keep him involved in the next season.

To follow up on the issue, Olivia and I met with Jack when his next set of color matching requests was completed. Jack was again unsatisfied with the colors—they were too light, too dark, too green, too yellow, etc. Since we had matched the colors under full color spectrum lighting and also cross-matched them against the suggested dye formulas, we were very surprised that Jack was still unhappy. He was adamant about discrepancies we couldn't see!

We asked more questions: Which ones were too dark? Which ones were too green? How many shades off was this one? But Jack kept giving us answers that didn't seem to correspond with the color swatches that we were looking at. Finally, I started asking broader questions: What were his real concerns about the colors? Did they have anything to do with the new production facilities where he would be placing his production? Was there any correlation between his concerns about color matching between the different fabrics in the line [TRUTH]?

The answers came out bit-by-bit. Gradually, Jack admitted that he was nervous about the expanding production base for the new collections. He was concerned about getting good color matches in the products produced by Britannia's different production locations. He was worried about whether the colors in different fabrics would match each other. Since the collections were meant to be sold and worn together, it was crucial for the colors of the tops and bottoms to match. Because it was especially hard to get knit and woven fabrics to match anyway, Jack had serious reservations about whether it was going to work with production facilities in various countries. When the design and development position was taken over by someone unknown to him, it only magnified his fears.

Because he'd been happy with the previous organizational structure, Jack was concerned that Olivia wouldn't be able to do the job as well. Feeling that the management transition was out of his control, Jack started clamping down on the elements he did have control over, such as the matching fabrics. After discussing his concerns and setting up a system for him to get more updates and input into the whole process, Jack felt included in the process. Our conversations helped him get to know Olivia better. And once he realized that he would still be consulted, he seemed relaxed and even cheerful.

When we mentioned his concerns about the colors, he shrugged and said the most amazing thing. "I'm color-blind!"

Olivia and I just stared at each other. We were flabbergasted. What about the shading differences, the colors that were too green or too red or just all together wrong? We'd been taking grief all this time from a guy who couldn't see color!

Now that he was feeling more comfortable, he confessed that he usually relied on his designers to tell him whether the colors matched or not and he would just parrot what they said. And then he smiled.

"Sometimes I just complain about the colors so you'll try harder and be more vigilant," he said. "But I don't know the difference myself! It's just my way of making sure things are going right."

From that day on, Jack was one of Olivia's biggest supporters and friends [PARTNER].

It turned out well, but it had been a potentially explosive situation. If Olivia hadn't gained the respect of the designers and merchandisers, her work would have always been questioned. Both Olivia and her team would have eventually burned out from overwork or left the company in frustration. The factories and suppliers would have become confused and annoyed at the impossible standards and expectations that they were to maintain. It was dramatic evidence of the power of asking the right questions and asking them soon.

Ask as many questions as you can—in as many ways as you can—and then do the best you can with what you've got. Adjust your strategy as you get new information. Be ready to sail straight ahead or tack as the wind shifts, always keeping your goals in sight.

> *The job is to ask questions—*
> *it always was—and to ask them*
> *as inexorably as I can.*
> *And to face the absence of precise answers*
> *with a certain humility.*
>
> —ARTHUR MILLER

THE WIENER QUESTION

Gay Hendricks, a renowned psychologist and friend, tells the story of the power of questions to solve what may seem to be unsolvable challenges:

> *Many years ago, I had dinner with Gregory Bateson, who told me how he came up with the double-bind theory of schizophrenia. He said he was visiting Norbert Wiener, the great cybernetic scientist at MIT.*
>
> *When he told Wiener he was working on schizophrenia, Wiener said something like "I'm an engineer and I don't know anything about schizophrenia, but if I were going to build a machine that makes people schizophrenic, what would the machine actually do?"*

Bateson immediately replied, "You'd build a machine that punished people when they were right." As soon as he said it, he suddenly understood the structure of schizophrenia.

The concept of asking how to generate the challenge you are facing is contrary to how we habitually think. We are usually focused on ways of solving the problem, not on how the problem was created in the first place. Herein lies the magic of asking questions outside the normal mindset and framework—asking questions from another perspective opens the door to the nature of the problem.

If you can comprehend how the dilemma was caused initially, you will have a better feel of how to resolve it. You will find out the elements and conditions that produced the problem in the first place. Once we recognize its under-pinnings, we can come up with an effective solution.

Live your questions now,
and perhaps even without knowing it,
you will live along some distant day
into your answers.

—RAINER MARIA RILKE

ACTION POINTS

1. Assume nothing.

2. Assess the situation.

3. Gather information and ask questions.

4. Integrate information and reassess the situation.

5. Ask more questions.

6. Compile all the data.

7. Plan and strategize actions.

8. Proceed mindfully and be prepared to adjust your course as new situations develop.

9. Keep asking questions all along the way.

CHAPTER ELEVEN

ONCE YOU GET INTO SOMETHING, DO IT 100%

HAVE YOU HEARD the old riddle: What is the difference between bacon and eggs? The chicken is interested but the pig is committed.

In life as well as in business, giving 100 percent makes a dramatic difference. Thankfully, our way of giving 100 percent doesn't involve life and limb, just to be fully present and dedicated to the project you have embarked on.

This one step—
choosing a goal and sticking to it—
changes everything.

—SCOTT REED

Steadfastness toward a goal is most often the only variable between success and failure. Thomas Edison is an inspiring example of someone who focused and worked diligently to achieve amazing goals. Edison was responsible for developing tremendous technology in his lifetime, as evidenced by his 1,093 patents. In his time, Edison was known as "The Wizard of Menlo Park."

His most famous invention, of course, was the incandescent lightbulb. But the phonograph, the kinetoscope (a small box for viewing films), as well as improvements on the stock ticker, the telegraph, and telephone were also attributable to Edison.

Despite his brilliance, Edison credited his incredible success to dedication and doggedness of purpose. Believing in hard work and his mission, he sometimes worked 20 hours a day [SWORD/MISTAKE]. His famous quote—"Genius is 1 percent inspiration and 99 percent perspiration"—tells us that no matter how great the idea or how many factors are in your favor, you still need to be 100 percent present to do the work.

Edison gave his all in his pursuit of new discoveries and was rewarded with wonderful results, as well as the respect and appreciation of the world. As a tribute to his contributions to humankind, all the electric lights in the United States were dimmed for one minute a few days after his death on October 18, 1931.

There is a Zen saying: "Before the enlightenment, chop wood and carry water, and after the enlightenment, chop wood and carry water." Chopping wood and carrying water are not very glamorous tasks. But practical tasks are what are required to make any vision a reality. The meaning of the saying to me is that, no matter how exciting or worthwhile the concept, you still have to do the actual work to get it done. Just having the thought or sketching a plan alone will not make the proposition a reality.

When I was growing up in Hong Kong, the fable of the Old Man and the Mountain was often told. It is a story about the value of sticking to a mission.

In a little village in China, an old man and his family lived in a small house facing a large mountain. His family had lived there for generations. The village periodically experienced drought and lean times because the mountain blocked the rain and sun from their farmland. One day, the old man decided that he could no longer live with the mountain and the threat of famine always in front of him. He wanted to put it behind him. He wanted to assure that his family did not have to suffer scarcity and starvation from crop failure anymore.

So the old man began his work. Every day he traveled with his rattan baskets to the base of the mountain, filled them with dirt, walked the small path all the way back to the clearing behind his house and dumped the dirt. It was a tiring, hot, and backbreaking task, but once he'd committed to it, he did it 100 percent every day. His family joined him. Every day, after they finished their work in the fields, they filled their baskets up with dirt from the mountain, carried them behind the little house, and dumped the dirt out—every day.

Soon the people in his small village noticed what they were doing and came to straighten the old man out. They didn't mince words. "You're crazy!" they said. "This mountain is huge. You'd need many lifetimes to move it." The old man nodded. "That's true," he said. "I will not see it moved in my lifetime and my children and grandchildren won't either. But one day my people will have put the mountain behind them [SWORD]."

The moral of the story is that if the cause is worthwhile, it is worth doing well. You should not be deterred by the challenges. Focus on your goal and it will be rewarded one day. Just don't give up and always do it 100 percent. You will achieve your dream.

> *Obstacles are those frightful things*
> *you see when you take your eyes*
> *off your goal.*
>
> —HENRY FORD

JUST ONE MORE AD

A different perspective on steadfastness of purpose is illustrated by the way the Internet and software industries used to look at marketing and sales. I observed this novel concept in my experience in the Internet and software business world in the late 1990s and early 2000s.

Many Internet and software companies in those times seemed to believe that all you had to do was to advertise and the sales would magically roll in. They appeared to have forgotten that companies had to have products that actually worked and were useful for there to be any customers, and that the products had to be priced commensurately with the amount that the companies valued them at. From my perspective, these were basic business concepts, but in this new Internet world there was a belief that these rules didn't apply [MISTAKE].

I was president of Fasturn at the time, and I was told by the advertising and PR companies we worked with that we were just not doing enough advertising. How could we expect to do any business if we didn't advertise more? Our business model of building strong and valuable online business negotiation tools seemed hopelessly old-fashioned to these hot new advertising and public relations firms. Even more remarkably, it seemed that other Internet companies and many software companies felt the same way. They had adopted the belief that once you had the publicity and had convinced potential customers of the hype, you could figure out what to sell them later. If the customers wanted something other than what your company was selling, you would simply say you had whatever it was that they wanted, then lock them into a contract while you worked to produce it.

There was neither a mission nor a purpose to the companies other than to raise more venture capital so that they could continue to develop various ideas and advertise them to see what would catch on in the current business craze. The people working in these companies appeared to be convinced that once they got a prospect interested, they could promise to produce anything. Their commitment to a project was as short-lived as the current buzz over what was hot in any given field. Companies changed names and business strategies every few months. Engineers and technicians were given new design requirements constantly.

There was no long-term focus. A company could be advertised as a business to consumer company (B2C) one week and morph into a business-to-business company (B2B) the next week. One week, the company's business was based on products for a certain part of the supply chain and two weeks later it was focused on a completely different part of the supply chain. The tides changed with whatever was rumored to be hot that week. The company's mission wasn't a factor.

Apparently, the peace of mind of the employees wasn't a factor either. This mode of operation was very stressful to the people working in these companies. There was no clear direction and no commitment to following a development path. The workers felt pushed and pulled, having to adjust and redo things frequently to try to conform to the strategy of the week.

Employees were lured to work in these companies with promises of huge upside gain in the company's stock options they were given. They were not committed to the purpose of the company, just to the dream of being on a winning team. Since the company had no central focus, the employees had no mission to align to and were, therefore, also not dedicated to the company. It was a case of people for themselves—a situation that did not promote any stability, collaboration, or innovation [MISTAKE].

Much of the potential for a significant leap forward through the use of the Internet was squandered because of this lack of long-term commitment and thinking. No one gave 100 percent commitment to any cause, and even though people were working 18-hour days, much of their efforts were wasted for lack of clarity and direction. Instead of sticking with their strength and expertise, many companies made constant changes in direction and damaged the credibility of Internet products. In the process, much effort and hundreds of millions of dollars were wasted.

Eventually, as we all know, the dot-com craze led to the dot-com crash. But it remains a very graphic example of how the lack of clear mission and dedication to staying the course can destroy so much potential value. Of the over 200-plus supply chain management technology firms that started at about the same time Fasturn did, less than 10 percent are still in business today. Sadly enough, many of the new companies had good ideas, but without perseverance and the dedication to a goal, they couldn't succeed. The rest of us missed out on the benefit of those products and services because of their short-term focus and lack of tenacity.

> *The person who makes a success of living*
> *is the one who sees his goal steadily*
> *and aims for it unswervingly.*
> *That is dedication.*

> —Cecil B. DeMille

In my career, the divisions I've managed were often times thousands of miles apart. People would remark on how exciting and glamorous my life must be—leaving the U.S.A. one day, landing in Seoul the next day, showing up in Shenzhen, China two days later.

In reality, my travel and work schedule was a fool-proof recipe for sleep deprivation and exhaustion from the jet lag and long work hours. I managed reasonably well under those conditions because I regarded every place as another step and as an additional opportunity to make direct progress toward my mission. Because I was committed to my purpose, I wanted to give my work full attention.

My business achievements are due, in large part, to my 100 percent commitment to whatever I was working on. When you are totally present, you are aware of all the elements that may influence or impact the situation. When you are alert to all aspects of the circumstances, you can respond appropriately and make more informed and effective decisions.

Devoting 100 percent to the job or situation at hand does not mean that you should be monofocused [MISTAKE]. To put your head down and keep doing things the same way with little rest will not get you innovative or superlative results. You run the risk of burning out, falling into a creative rut, and not being aware of additional input and resources that may make your task much easier.

In each work or life situation, I did my best to maintain life balance; whether learning how to sleep on planes, doing stretching exercises in hotel rooms, eating a healthy diet, meditating everyday, or e-mailing family and friends, it's critical to the job and critical to a healthy, balanced life.

HEAL THYSELF, HEAL THE WORLD

Having a healthy, balanced life is essential for superior results. You cannot be fully engaged in your work if you are tired or worried about something else. Part of you will still be occupied with feelings of weariness, no matter how you try to block them out.

The safety announcement on every airplane flight says it so well: "Put your own oxygen mask on before you help others with their masks." If you are not taking care of yourself, you are not able to be truly ready to take care of others. You cannot give fully if there is a drain in your personal system, just as a bucket with a leak cannot be totally filled.

The grass is not always greener
on the other side of the fence.
The grass is greenest where it is watered.
When crossing over fences, carry water with you
and tend the grass wherever you may be.

—Robert Fulghum

When I was at Aveda, I saw this point illustrated every day with employees who believed passionately in the company mission, the enthusiasm and commitment to the work was always strong. Aveda's employees were zealous in working hard and in spreading the word about the company and its products. They were ardent advocates of Aveda [PARTNER] and wanted to share the benefits and goodness of Aveda's philosophy and its products [PARTNERS] with as many people as they could. People would come to work early and stay late to finish projects.

Walking the halls late at night, I would see most office and lab lights on. There were teams deep in discussion about how to use different organic essential oils for the products, how to get the healing message of the products across to consumers, and how to create new products that answer consumers' needs. The Aveda scientists would be testing the efficacy of various plants and flower components for healing and life enhancement late into the night.

Inspired by the stories about the dedication and never give up attitude of the founder, they tried to emulate Horst's entrepreneurial spirit, neglecting everything else in their lives. They were so focused and attached to their specific tasks that they were frequently not able to incorporate new data or work in a collaborative way with others.

They took a narrow part of Horst's bigger story and made it the only option [MISTAKE].

As a result of this manner of operating, they were generating many new products, but not necessarily the best products for the company. Sometimes the products were too specific to be popularly received by the consumers—too narrowly focused—like the people who designed them.

When I came to the company, I found a high staff turnover. People would stay for a while, wholeheartedly committed to the work, and then gradually, with little explanation, many of them would leave. It was puzzling and worrisome. Horst and I wanted to give the people who were giving so much energy and love to the creation of products the same care and consideration they were giving the company.

We discovered that people came to the company with great ideals. They were enamored with the company's mission of producing products that were good for people inside and out and were healthy for the planet, combined with the fact that Aveda also gave fair compensation to the original source of the ingredients, which made the company an ideal place for them to work. Their desire to contribute to this vision was so strong that some of them neglected other facets of their lives, such as their personal health, family, and friends [MISTAKE].

This singular focus created a lot of stress in their lives. Soon they were not as productive or as happy as they were when they started. Their work deteriorated as a result. Some realized what was happening and made adjustments. But others spiraled down until one day they decided to leave the company. The joy and the passion they had when they came into the company had been eaten up by the myopic concentration on the task instead of the whole picture. It was a loss for everyone—the employee, his or her family, and the company.

When we realized what was happening, we gathered the team together for several brainstorming sessions to change the environment so that it would nourish each person's creativity and productivity. The key, we felt, was to remind each individual that everything is connected; nothing works well in a vacuum [TRUTH]. The ones who had learned how to balance their lives shared their insights with the group, and everyone participated in developing a strategy that would support the whole team.

Various new initiatives came into effect. Yoga classes were offered at lunchtime. We explored and supported avenues of childcare. Suggestions were made for personal and professional development opportunities. Employees were encouraged to involve their families and friends in the company's progress. Areas for workers to relax, contemplate, and exercise indoors and outdoors were expanded, giving them additional locales to exchange ideas and to connect. Suggestion boxes were situated in the various parts of the facility [TRUTH] and the company's comments and actions were posted in the employee newsletters for people to see and respond to. (Aveda already had a delicious organic cafeteria so that everyone could enjoy low cost healthy meals. We wanted the team [PARTNER] to feel that they were fed mind, body, and spirit.)

Happily, I can report that the rewards of the programs were extremely positive and gratifying. Turnover reduced dramatically, work performance and productivity improved, and a higher level of positivism prevailed in the company. The employees worked hard and were fully present when they were at work. They were not overly

tired or worried about their personal lives, since they were no longer slighting the issues in their lives for the sake of the company. Absenteeism went down and the feedback from our customers was even more glowing than before.

Before long, when I walked down the halls to leave at night, mine would be one of the few lights still left on. Since I commuted to Aveda's Minneapolis headquarters from California, I worked late while I was in town. It was my way of creating life balance, working hard for two weeks and then having more flextime when I was telecommuting from home. Life balance became a working model at Aveda. And as I expected, the company grew even faster once we truly lived the philosophy of honoring the total being; the company's sales and the employees benefited.

As you can see, it takes more than just determined effort to accomplish your mission. It takes a dedication to purpose along with an acknowledgement of the wholeness of your being and life. Working hard and diligently on the goal is needed, but it is also important to respect and balance the other aspects of your life—physical health, emotional health, spiritual health, family, and friends.

ACTION POINTS

Once you commit to a mission, devote 100 percent to the purpose—but remember to keep your life in balance:

1. Align with your mission.

2. Define your venture.

3. Determine viability of strategy.

4. Ensure that your plan is in line with your purpose.

5. Gather resources to make your plan a reality.

6. Commit yourself wholeheartedly to the project.

7. Remember to maintain life balance.

8. Persevere and adjust with new input.

9. Have fun in the process.

CHAPTER TWELVE

DON'T BE "DO OR DIE"

Have Vision but Be Flexible

AFTER ALMOST FOUR YEARS of work in Hong Kong with Britannia Sportswear, I had had enough. I was ready to leave Hong Kong and go home to the United States. The work was getting more frustrating. The joy and satisfaction I had once derived from doing well and doing good at the same time seemed almost impossible to achieve at work anymore.

The company had grown a lot in physical size, business volume, and personnel over the years, but the market was rapidly changing, putting the company structure into question. Fashion trends were shifting. New competitors had entered the market niche that Britannia so carefully cultivated. And it was getting harder and harder to predict which fabrics, styles, colors, and quantities the retailers would purchase.

As each division of Britannia began fighting for survival, they started competing with each other instead of collaborating as a company [MISTAKE]. Each one was clamoring for special attention and demanding extensions on deadlines.

Since our team in Hong Kong was the development and production center of the whole operation, it fell onto our shoulders to sort out the conflicting directives of the different divisions. One day we would get an order to dye a million yards of denim fabric a light blue. The next week we would get two new orders—one from one division asking to change half the order to a darker shade and another from another division demanding that all the denim be dyed in another shade. Sorting out who had the final authority was a constant debate; each division wanted to ensure that they had the right fabric for their production. Each one claimed power.

Going back to the dye houses and fabric manufacturers to ask for yet another modification in our orders and further extensions in commitment, timing was increasingly difficult. And the work ethic was changing. Pledges being made to manufacturers were conveniently forgotten. Factories were being pressured to give more and more price reductions and quicker deliveries in return for continuing business. Our credibility as a company, as well as my personal reputation, was being eroded with each broken promise and unreasonable, last minute changes.

Working at the company began to gnaw at my insides. I knew I was not working in alignment with my mission anymore. As the frontline face to many of the factories and manufacturers, I felt uncomfortable having to execute directions that conflicted with my personal ethics of fair play and honesty. So I decided to resign. I would settle happily back in California and look for a new job then [SWORD].

When I met with the CEO to tender my resignation, he asked numerous questions. I told him honestly why I was leaving and offered suggestions [TRUTH] on how to alleviate the tension that had been building in the company.

Much to my surprise, he agreed with many of my assessments, but he also acknowledged that it would be very tricky to try to change it at the time. Too many egos were involved and he did not feel that he could jeopardize his company in making such significant reporting realignments. It was a sad moment for me; I felt that an opportunity to do the right thing was being passed by.

When I told him I'd be returning to California, he surprised me with an offer to start a new division in Los Angeles. Although he didn't feel able to change the existing branches of the company, he was eager for me to apply my insights and philosophy to start a new division. Since I had only wanted to leave the company because of the growing ethical and philosophical problems that were developing, his offer neatly resolved my conflict.

The division he offered me would make shoes to coordinate with Britannia's clothes. It would be called Brittsport Shoes. It would enable me to revitalize my former shoe manufacturing contacts, use my shoe industry know-how, and reenergize Britannia with a new line of products as well. It was a win-win situation for everyone.

I was thrilled to be given a chance to make a difference. I saw it as an opportunity to participate in the revival of the company and even improve the strained vendor relationships that had once been so solid.

Had I made up my mind to leave the company no matter what, I would not have been flexible enough to see this for the exciting opportunity it was. I did not have to leave the company to fulfill my dream. Being willing to listen and incorporate new data into my plan, I had the delight of staying on to do what I could to restore Britannia to its former glory.

Life takes twists and turns all the time. If you remain centered in what you believe, you can adapt to the circumstances and not let the outside conditions knock you off-course and prevent you from reaching your goals. Staying anchored in your purpose [SWORD], you can decide how to integrate the new factors into your decision making process.

HIGH OCTANE ADAPTABILITY

No one stakes more on their ability to adapt quickly to change, while keeping their focus on the goal, than racecar drivers. Since Britannia designed and supplied the team outfits for the Flying Tiger (Air) Line Racing Team, I had the opportunity to watch the races from the pit stops at the Macau Grand Prix and to ask some of the drivers what it meant to put so much on the line for their goals.

I was mesmerized by the speed, skill, and presence of mind of the drivers. I used to watch those races in awe, holding my breath and plugging my ears—holding my breath from the excitement and fear of being so close to the powerful machines going at unbelievably high-speeds, screeching around corners verging on being out of control; and plugging my ears from the deafening roar of the engines, nervous and scared that I might hear the terrifying sound of screaming brakes and crunching metal. It was an exhausting, but exhilarating way to spend a few days.

The most amazing thing to me about those spectacular feats of speed and control was the incredible focus and determination of the drivers. These world-class racers would strap themselves into virtual land rockets and blast off, driving around the track at velocities that I dreaded even dreaming about.

When I asked them how they could do it—when every time they got behind the wheel, they ran the risk of being on their last ride—their answers had a theme that shouldn't have surprised me. They said they stayed *present, alert, focused on the goal, and ready to adjust instantly.* And each of them was perfectly clear that if they didn't love what they were doing, the risks wouldn't be worthwhile.

Whether you're racing in the Grand Prix, trying to build your business, or live a more rewarding life, the same guidelines apply:

BE PRESENT AND ALERT.

Whatever it is that you are doing, it pays to be aware of all factors involved. How mindful and observant you are will determine whether you catch the vital clues or miss them. Being alert to all the signs may mean the difference between success and failure.

If a Grand Prix driver were to be inattentive for even an instant, he may miss another car pulling up alongside him. And if he were to unknowingly steer to that side, the mistake could be fatal for both drivers.

Being alert and mindful means taking into account all the factors that could influence the outcome of any plan. In everyday life, a sigh, a look, or a casual comment may be indicators that reveal how a discussion or negotiation is developing. An unexpected variation in production, delivery, or sales may give you important data about the trend or viability of the project. It's all there if you heed the signs by being present and alert.

Focus on the goal.

By now you know that this one is of paramount importance. If you have no goal, no mission, you are mindlessly "doing," with no long-term plan or reason for being. There can be no passion or dedication to the business at hand. If a racecar driver was not determined to win the race, there would be little incentive for him to practice, strategize, and keep himself in good health. The same is true for you.

Once you have found your mission, commit to it. Then let every action you take reinforce your focus on the goal.

Be ready to adjust instantly.

As the racecar driver rounds the corner, ready to accelerate on the straight stretch, he is prepared for any eventuality. A spun-out car may block the path or it may be clear for him to really step on the gas and gain on his competitors. He may use that stretch as an opportunity to rush into the pit and get his car fixed before he can continue. He is always prepared to modify his plans as new information comes in.

Much like the driver, as you forge ahead in your quest, always keep your eyes on your goal but be ready to adjust to anything new you encounter. Being prepared and flexible will help you recover from unexpected changes and even take advantage of new circumstances that develop. Failing to take the shifting state of affairs into account can only create disappointment and frustration, since yesterday's solution may not work on today's problem.

Love what you're doing or the risks aren't worthwhile.

The racecar driver has such a passion for racing that he's willing to take the risk that it may, literally, cost him his life. How much passion do you have for your work? Or, for your life?

Everything in life entails a choice. Why not choose something that you have a real passion for? If you are aligned with your life mission, it is a sure way to ensure that you are in the flow of what calls to you. Otherwise, you will have a high probability of feeling that you paid too high of a price in time, energy, and resources to pursue something that gives you little inner peace.

ACTION POINTS

1. Stay focused on your mission.

2. Assess the current strategy to ensure you are in line with your mission.

3. Adjust and fine-tune your plan as necessary.

4. Devote 100 percent to your refined action steps.

5. Enjoy and learn from the current process.

6. Be proud of where you are and what you are doing.

As you wander on through life, sister/brother,
whatever be your goal,
keep your eye upon the donut,
and not upon the hole.

— SIGN IN THE MAYFLOWER COFFEE SHOP,
CHICAGO

CHAPTER THIRTEEN

FORGET ABOUT GLASS CEILINGS, WORRY ABOUT GLASS WALLS

GLASS CEILINGS are the proverbial barriers to success for women and other minorities. Being both a woman and a minority, I'm here to tell you that it isn't the glass ceilings you should worry about—it's the glass walls.

The path to advancement is first sideways, not up. If you are trained or have expertise in only one area, you will not be able to rise to any position of significance in a company. The higher you go in a company, the more diverse and comprehensive an understanding of the whole operation you need. When you get to the top—past the "glass ceiling"—it will mean you have already gone through all the glass walls of the different operational areas in a company.

CARLY S. FIORINA, CEO OF HEWLETT-PACKARD

Let's track the career path of the woman who's been rated by *Fortune* magazine as "The Most Powerful Woman in American Business" for the years 2000–2002, and see how she rose to the top. Carly S. Fiorina was the CEO of Hewlett-Packard (HP), which after its acquisition of Compaq Computer Corporation had a combined revenue on a pro forma basis of approximately $81.1 billion in fiscal 2001, with operations in more than 160 countries.

To make it to that position, Carly had to have incredible versatility. But Carly was used to that. She had had to learn to adjust to a variety of situations early on in life. When she was a child, her family moved so often that she went to five high schools. She became skilled at adapting to change and managed to do very well in school. After graduating with a Bachelor's degree in Medieval History and Philosophy, Carly went on to get a Master's degree in Business Administration, and then a Master of Science degree. Along the way, she acquired good judgment and the many abilities that prepared her for business success.

In her work life prior to the top job at HP, she stayed nearly 20 years at AT&T and Lucent. But within those years, she made lateral moves into different divisions as she climbed the corporate ranks. She began her career with AT&T as a sales account executive and progressed rapidly, developing a reputation for savvy marketing and sales techniques.

After doing well in AT&T's core long-distance business, she made a radical shift to the Network Systems Group, the sleepy telephone equipment manufacturing business. Working there, she expanded her knowledge of the whole telecommunications industry and excelled in what had always been a staid arena of telephone equipment manufacturing. Indeed, she thrived in every area of the company. She became AT&T's first female officer at age 35 and was heading the North American operations at 40.

Then, as president of Lucent's Global Service Provider Business, she dramatically increased its growth rate, its international revenues, and market share in every region across every product line. In addition, she led the planning and execution of Lucent's 1996 initial public offering and subsequent spin-off from AT&T, one of the largest and most successful IPOs ever.

According to *BusinessWeek Online,* when the leaders of HP were looking for a new CEO, each search committee member detailed 20 qualities they would like to see in the new CEO. Then they narrowed it down to four essential criteria which, as it happened, perfectly matched Carly's diverse background and experience: "the ability to conceptualize and communicate sweeping strategies, the operations savvy to deliver on quarterly financial goals, the power to bring urgency to an organization, and the management skills to drive a nascent Net vision throughout the company."

The CEO search committee looked at 300 potential candidates. "Carly was the best," says Sam Ginn, chairman of the HP board's nominating and governance committee. "We see her being HP's CEO for a very long time."

The reason Carly won over the other 299 candidates was, in part, due to her ability to take on new challenges, quickly assess the situation, and devise effective solutions. She has the ability to lead and integrate input from a variety of sources because she has deep experience of doing so in many departments and locations. Her history of crossing over the glass walls gave her the diversity and depth of knowledge to manage, lead, and inspire a world-class operation. She is a clear example of how someone can go through the glass ceiling because she's already learned how—by going through all the glass walls.

FROM TRENDY CLOTHES TO POTS AND PANS

Looking back at my own career, I can see how my thirst for learning and excelling in a variety of areas helped me move ahead of others who may have had a narrower, but deeper, focus in a particular field. I do believe that my desire to accomplish something new has been instrumental in advancing my whole career path. In fact, I think this same aspiration to be different and to do atypical things was what propelled me into my first job with May Department Stores California.

During the interview, the recruiter asked me what department in the store I was interested in. Not wanting to give an impression of being totally ignorant about the retail business as a career, I tried to give an answer that showed more thought than I actually had given it. (I was just interviewing with May Department Stores California as a "practice interview." Because I'd never gone on a professional job interview before, I thought I'd practice with a company in a field that I knew nothing about. That way, it wouldn't hurt my chances with a company in a field I was really interested in.)

As I thought about the recruiter's question, I scanned the typical departments of a retail store in my mind. Because of my youth, I thought the most obvious choice would be junior sportswear where I shopped for trendy clothes. But I suspected that would be regarded a predictable, unimaginative answer. The only other area I knew much about was the department where the exotic carvings, beautiful crystals, and exquisite "objet d'art" were displayed. I used to like to stroll through that area and wonder how those rare handicraft items from foreign places got there. Thinking that would be a good place to learn something new, I blurted out, "Housewares!" (I didn't find out till later that the housewares department sold pots and pans.)

But despite my confusion, my interest in an unexpected department of the store may have set me apart from the other applicants and given me an advantage. One of the trainers in the May Executive Training Program that I had joined said she was surprised to see me list housewares as my favorite department. She said that it caught her eye and made her interested in getting to know me a bit more.

After I entered the executive training program, I continued to pursue as wide a range of experiences as possible. I worked in budget men's sportswear, bedding and linens, junior sportswear, boulevard dresses, young men's sportswear, and hosiery, footwear, and bodywear. Eager to learn all the intricacies of a department store, I moved cartons and pallets of goods; set up floor layouts; dealt with the warehouse and receiving department; worked with the accounting and receivables area; pitched in with the display, marketing, and advertising departments; worked the sales floor; and gradually became proficient at buying, designing, and importing goods. In the process, I developed my management skills and found out how to motivate and enlist others in a common mission.

By the time Britannia Sportswear offered me a post in Hong Kong to build a design and development department for the international jeans company, I was ready. I was eager to have a chance to learn something new, go to a new place, and gain additional skills and know-how. Britannia was interested in me because I had already shown, in my relatively young career, how I was willing, able, and happy to learn, adapt, and innovate to create superior solutions to meet the company's goals.

Going from the retail business to Britannia Sportswear's design and manufacturing environment, I added an extra dimension to my knowledge base. Being able to handle work in both wholesale and retail made me a valuable resource in two different industries. Within those industries, I have also successfully held a multitude of positions: store management, retail buying, designing, merchandising, importing, exporting, production planning, manufacturing, marketing, and sales. In my quest to learn and to improve I have enhanced my value to any potential employer, as well as to myself, as an entrepreneur.

I have sought out and looked at every new opportunity asking whether it took me toward my goal of improving and learning skills. Seeking to better myself, I have volunteered to help in other departments, always asking questions and observing how others achieve success—always ready to seek and absorb their wisdom and expertise.

To me, failure is only a sign that there must be another way of accomplishing my goals. I forge onward. With my mission as my anchor [SWORD], I am grounded and ready to try again. I regard each position as a place to learn, to gain competence, and to give back 100 percent to the company who had the faith in my abilities to hire me to perform the job for them.

When I look back on my career now, I am grateful for the opportunity to have participated and contributed to a rich variety of businesses. This broad base of experience has given me the strategic perspective to be able to assess a situation and integrate multiple sources of data into a functional and effective strategy and to enlist others into the mission. Having been involved with the whole range of ventures—from start-ups to multinationals, from roaring successes to struggling operations—I am ready to respond with urgency and sensitivity to decision making, always executing my tasks in a timely manner.

The array of industries in both wholesale and retail of apparel, footwear, home furnishings, the Internet, publishing, and software businesses that I have had the good fortune to work in, have given me an abundance of expertise. Glass ceilings are not as hard to break if you have the right equipment and tools to crack them.

In the twenty-first century, each person will have an average of six careers in their lifetime. Prepare now to learn, grow, and move from department to department, from division to division, from company to company, and from industry to industry. Do your best in each position, give it 100 percent, learn, collaborate, create, innovate, inspire, share, and enjoy the journey.

ACTION POINTS

1. Review your mission, goals, and the skills you need to achieve it.

2. Take stock of your current skill and knowledge base.

3. Learn and excel in your current field.

4. Enlist the support and guidance of mentors and other wisdom leaders.

5. Survey company/environs for areas in which you can contribute and participate.

6. Add value to the identified field(s) by active participation.

7. Seek to transfer to sectors in which you have had less exposure.

8. Repeat 3, 4, and 5 until you have the comprehensive knowledge base crucial to your goal.

9. Enjoy the ride to the top!

I am still learning.

—MICHELANGELO

CHAPTER FOURTEEN

DON'T WAIT 'TIL YOU KNOW HOW TO DO SOMETHING

Learn It on the Run!

HAVE YOU EVER SAID, "I'll do that as soon as I . . ." Fill in the blanks for the balance of that sentence—"learn how to do it really well," "practice another six months," "get really prepared." The common refrain here is that you hope to do it later, when you feel more confident and better equipped [MISTAKE].

Don't wait. Do it now. You will never be as ready as you feel that you should be. You will always have a bit of anxiety when you do something challenging, whether it is for the first time or the fiftieth time. It's natural and actually desirable—extra adrenaline keeps you alert and more attuned to what you are doing. You perform better under a hint of stress than when you are too complacent.

I know what you are thinking: "But you don't understand. I get paralyzed by fear when I speak in front of groups!" Or, "If I'm not totally ready for the new position, I'll fail miserably." I do understand, but I repeat, you will never be ready for something until you do it.

Loretta LaRoche, a well-known stress management consultant and author, advocates that you do the things that you would like to do and not agonize over the details. She titled her book, *Life Is Not a Stress Rehearsal: Bringing Yesterday's Sane Wisdom into Today's Insane World.* I think the title says it all.

> *Never be afraid to try something new.*
> *Remember, amateurs built the Ark.*
> *Professionals built the Titanic.*
>
> —ANONYMOUS

When you are grounded in your mission and you understand the bigger picture, things that might otherwise be scary or daunting become more comfortable to tackle. When there is a deeper reason for being, the actual process of getting there will seem more approachable. This has been my experience all my life. When I have a cause I'm committed to, achieving it becomes much more important to me than the obstacles in the way.

We have all read about how people perform superhuman feats when something really vital is at stake, such as a mother lifting a car to pull her child out from under the wheel. Normally she would not have the strength, but she puts that obstacle aside on behalf of something so much more important to her that the obstacle isn't even worth considering. Her mission is to save her child and that means much more to her than the conventional thinking about size, weight, and strength.

How do you parlay this wisdom into bettering our lives and our work? By knowing that when you are focused on your mission, you can stretch and excel beyond what your fears would have you believe. To achieve and grow at work or in other aspects of life, you have to take risks—calculated, well-thought-out risks.

FOLLOW THE MISSION, SKIP A GRADE

Ever since I found my mission at 11-years-old, I've been attempting new challenges toward my goal while acknowledging my fears along the way. I screened every decision and action of any significance through that ultimate purpose.

Being an impatient person, I was eager to start making a difference as soon as I could, but the years of schooling seemed to stretch on forever. Deciding that I should try to shorten the education process, I started looking for other options. When a schoolmate of mine transferred to another school that she claimed would accelerate the education process, I applied there immediately.

I applied for a grade higher than I was in. Since I was anxious to save the world, the sooner I could get going the better. Skipping a grade made perfect sense. Then my fears kicked in: What if it was too hard and I flunked out? What if I didn't flunk out but just squeaked by? How could I save the world if I didn't learn everything well enough? After being in all-girl schools, how would I behave around boys? What would my parents think when I told them I had applied to another school?

Not only fears, but also solid arguments stood against my transferring to another school. But I was willing to take the risk for what I saw as a way to achieve my goal sooner. I would study hard and adjust to the new environment if they would accept me to the school. My parents should have been happy that I was trying to improve my education. I was strengthened and centered in knowing that, whatever the outcome, I was following the right course for me. By pursuing my mission and taking an opportunity to accelerate the process, I was listening to my inner wisdom and doing what called to me [SWORD].

Happily, the school accepted me, and after a difficult initial few months, I managed to do very well. I even left early for college before finishing high school. And the boys were okay. I didn't have much time for them because I was too busy studying, participating in sports, and singing in the school choir.

What I learned from that experience has helped me throughout life. If you have a core mission [TRUTH], the steps to get there will show up. You may have to stretch and take courage to leverage your wisdom and assets, but take the plunge. You can't swim if you don't get in the water and try.

The more you seek security, the less of it you have.
But the more you seek opportunity, the more likely
it is that you will achieve the security
that you desire.

—BRIAN TRACY

DROP OUT
AND LEAP FORWARD

Michael Dell started Dell Computers in 1984 in his dorm room with $1,000. While still in high school, Michael got his first computer. Taking it apart, he realized that based on the cost of the components, there was a huge profit margin in the computer business. Researching further, he found that there were many inefficiencies, which made the prices much higher than they had the potential to be. He saw the need for an efficient system of serving the growing market of people who wanted value-priced, customized computers. And he felt he could deliver it to them. He had a vision that he could provide better service at cheaper prices more quickly than IBM, the megalith industry leader run by executives and computer engineers with infinitely more training and experience than he had. This was an audacious belief for a 19-year-old who soon became a college dropout to test his theory [SWORD].

Michael leapt into the new and unknown world of business and Internet sales with nothing more than his own conviction. You can imagine that his family and friends must have had serious misgivings about his decision to drop out of the University of Texas to do what no one had done before—especially with no money and no experience. But Michael knew he could make a difference in the way computers were sold and marketed.

And he was right. Michael Dell created a company that defied convention. It marketed, sold, and delivered products to the consumers as no one had before. Selling computers directly to consumers, he bypassed middlemen and retailers. Dell was the first computer company to sell them over the Internet. Now it does up to half of its sales via the Web.

At every step of the way, there was no guarantee that Michael was going to succeed. There couldn't be—he was forging a path that no one had taken before. By stretching himself and his company to innovate and risk, he created something that had previously been only in his mind. And despite his fears of failure, and in the face of everyone else's doubt, he made it real. The experience has given him the courage to continue to step out and tread where no one has before, conceiving and executing new strategies to further his goal of serving the consumer better, faster, and cheaper [SWORD].

Today, benefiting from efficiencies created in part by Dell's Web-based supply chain, the company has remained profitable, even as it has cut into its competition by lowering its prices to such a degree that it started a PC price war.

Again, Michael Dell has broken out of the security of the mold. With the economy suffering from the effects of the dot-com crash and the general economic slowdown, in addition to the lingering effects of September 11, it was an unlikely time for a company to reduce their prices. There were great hazards involved in the price reductions, since it was possible that they would not be offset by additional volume. What if consumers were reluctant to buy more computers in uncertain economic times—regardless of the new lower prices? If there was ever a time for Michael to say, "I'll do that as soon as . . ."—the economy picks up, the profit margin increases, the consumers show an increased interest"—this is it. But the price cuts were instituted anyway and Michael's strategy is succeeding.

Dell's market share is going up and they are able to maintain profitability from increased volume and efficiencies.

In 2001, according to *BusinessWeek Online,* Dell connected 90 percent of its suppliers into its production system via the Internet so they could have up-to-the-minute information on orders and replenish Dell's supplies on a just-in-time basis. This enabled Dell to drastically reduce their inventory to a five days' supply last year—down from 13 days in 1997—and save $50 million. In comparison, rival Compaq Computer Corporation had more than three weeks of inventory on hand last quarter. Once again, Michael was taking his company to new frontiers that no business had ever been before; he continues to explore and take calculated chances everyday.

His latest strategy is to encourage customers to adopt Web-based procurement systems that can hook directly into Dell's order management system. This produces timesavings for the buyer and Dell, plus it gives Dell more insight into its customers' needs. Dell secures loyal customers and also more effective planning information. It's another win-win and it's something new that no one has done before.

In 2002, Dell Computer ranked 53rd on the *Fortune* 500 Company list, ahead of such giants as UPS, Motorola, Dow Chemical, and Pepsi. Michael Dell, with a net worth of more than $11 billion, ranks 18th on the *Forbes'* list of richest people in the world. He accomplished all this by being courageous and going where he had never been before—by following his mission. He didn't wait to make sure it was possible or follow someone else's example. By believing in himself and his purpose, he lived his dream [SWORD].

Years ago, I was talking to Barbara De Angelis, a dear friend of mine, and confided to her that I was nervous about speaking in front of a crowd of 5,000 people because it was a larger crowd than I had ever addressed before. She laughed and said, "What are you going to do? Practice your speech in front of another group of 5,000 people first?" There is always going to be a first time. You can't practice everything beforehand. Sometimes, you just have to jump in and do it.

I have mainly succeeded in all my leaps and when I haven't accomplished my project right away, I took the lesson [MISTAKE] as an opportunity to learn how to do it better next time. This concept has added to my experience base and made me a stronger and more knowledgeable person as a result.

ACTION POINTS

1. Reexamine your mission.

2. Center your thoughts and goals on it.

3. Explore the avenues of fulfilling your mission.

4. Research and prepare for action.

5. Enlist help and support.

6. Follow through with enthusiasm and courage.

7. Stay present, honest, and engaged in your project.

8. Learn and adapt as the situation unfolds.

9. Have fun in the process.

My attitude is that if you push me toward something that you think is a weakness, then I will turn that perceived weakness into a strength.

—MICHAEL JORDAN

Don't Wait 'Til You Know How to Do Something

CHAPTER FIFTEEN

Make a Difference, One Starfish at a Time

THE STORY OF THE STARFISH is one that has helped me through times when I despaired over whether I was making a positive difference in the world. It is especially meaningful to me because I heard it from my beloved mentor Robert Muller, who was for more than 30 years the Assistant Secretary General for the United Nations.

One day a man was walking on the beach in the late afternoon at low tide. A summer storm had passed through earlier that day and left the air crisp and clear. He smiled as he walked, enjoying the beauty of the day and long expanse of deserted beach that seemed to stretch on for miles.

In the distance, he could see a lone figure walking toward him. Every few steps, the stranger bent over to pick something up and throw it into the water. As the man got closer to the stranger, he could see that they were starfish. The beach was littered with them after the storm. He had been so caught up in his own thoughts that he hadn't even noticed them. But they were scattered down the length of the beach as far as the eye could see.

"What are you doing?" the man asked the stranger.

The stranger carefully plucked another starfish from the sand. "I'm returning the starfish to their home so they'll live."

"But there must be thousands of starfish on this beach, maybe even tens of thousands! What difference can you make?"

The stranger smiled and flung the starfish out into the sea. "I made a difference to that one," he said.

Inspired by the man with the starfish, Robert has applied the same purpose to his own life in what he calls "The Cleanest Mile." Wherever he goes, he picks up debris and cleans a mile. When he is at home in Costa Rica, he cleans the mile on his daily walk to his office at the University for Peace. When he goes to the cemetery, where his first wife rests, he cleans a mile. He has been doing it for more than 20 years, ever since he started this tradition on his daily walk to the train station in New York.

Two years ago, while Robert was in Sardinia, Italy, he cleaned the beach near his hotel before his address to the International Conference on Globalization and the Fate of the Nation-State. At the press conference afterward, he was asked how a single person could make any difference. He recounted his story of the starfish and the beach cleanup he had done that morning. The story was printed in *Il Messaggero*, the leading Italian newspaper. It so inspired people that 120,000 volunteers cleaned 200 Italian beaches that week. Five hundred young environmentalists met from nine Mediterranean countries and started the Clean Up the Mediterranean Sea Project that same summer. Another program funded by the Italian Region called Clean Beaches is now a permanent project in Italy. And it all started with one man cleaning a mile [PARTNERS].

When you make a difference, whether it is one starfish at a time or one piece of debris at a time, the ripple effect is magical. It may not be creating global change. It may not make you the richest person in the world. And it may not be the thing that wins you a Nobel Prize. But it will have a positive impact. And in the end, that's all we can do—make change one step, one person at a time.

All it takes to make a difference
is the courage to stop proving I was right
in being unable to make a difference . . .
to stop assigning the cause for my inability
to the circumstances outside myself
and to be willing to have been that way,
and to see that the fear of being a failure is
a lot less important than the unique opportunity
I have to make a difference.

—WERNER ERHARD

CARPET WEAVER, WORLD CHANGER

Another story that sustains me is the story of Iqbal Masih. Iqbal was a Pakistani little boy who was sold to a carpet factory owner by his parents for the equivalent of $12 when he was 4 years old. For the next six years, while he was literally shackled to the weaving loom, he wove carpets, tying little knots at all hours of the day and night. When he was ten, he escaped. He found refuge at the Bonded Labor Liberation Front of Pakistan and spent the next two years helping free other bonded labor children from his same fate.

I was privileged to meet Iqbal when he came to the United States to accept the first Reebok Youth In Action Award in 1994. I was on the board of Reebok Human Rights Awards, which gave Iqbal this tribute, not only for freeing other children, but also for bringing to international attention the suffering of countless children who were being enslaved to make carpets. He vowed to use his prize money to pay for schooling so that he could become a lawyer to help more people.

Sadly, less than a year after he returned to Pakistan, 12-year-old Iqbal was assassinated. Mr. Kahn, President of the Bonded Labor Liberation Front of Pakistan, said that Iqbal had received many death threats from angry members of the carpet industry who wanted to silence him [TRUTH/SWORD]. Iqbal's campaign had already led to the closure of dozens of carpet weaving factories in his district. But his untimely death did not end the movement he started.

An article about Iqbal's life and death caught the eye

of another 12-year-old in Ontario, Canada. Craig Kielburger was motivated by Iqbal's crusade and determined to carry his work forward. Craig founded Free the Children, a youth organization with the mission: "To free children from poverty, exploitation, and abuse and to give children a voice, leadership training, and opportunities to take action on issues which affect them from a local to an international level."

In 1996, two years after Iqbal's receipt of the Reebok Youth In Action Award, Craig Kielburger won that same award. Craig had carried the torch that the young Pakistani boy lit by helping others, one at a time, to be free from horrible abuse. Iqbal's actions had become widely known. The people who killed him thought his death would put an end to his work, but Iqbal's spirit surged forward.

Now, Craig and his organization have multiplied Iqbal's message of hope and youthful social activism to 35 countries all over the world. Free the Children is dedicated to eliminating the exploitation of children around the world by encouraging youth to volunteer in, as well as to create, programs and activities that relieve the plight of underprivileged children. What a legacy that a small, 12-year-old, illiterate boy from an impoverished part of the world has given us!

The remarkable spirit of these boys is proof that indeed one person can make a difference, one person at a time. Doing what I can with gratitude and devotion, I trust that every step, every good deed, is adding to the magic of healing and bettering the world that we share.

You, too, can find solace in knowing that whatever good you choose to do is resonating in the world, creating more good than you may ever know.

ACTION POINTS

1. Anchor your service work in your mission.

2. Combine and synergize your ability to generate revenue and give back to the world.

3. Celebrate and focus on what you can do.

4. Be grateful for the good.

5. Acknowledge the positive and be comforted that you are making a beneficial difference.

I think the purpose of life is to be useful,
to be responsible, to be honorable, to be compassionate.
It is, after all, to matter, to count, to stand for something,
to have made some difference that you lived at all.

—LEO C. ROSTEN

EPILOGUE

Here we are at the end of the book. What words of wisdom can I leave with you? What nugget of information will transmit the magic to ensure your success and happiness?

Well, it's simple. Never forget that you have everything you need inside of you. You are enough.

Can you do some more polishing of the jewel that is you? Probably. Can you build on your strengths, hone your skills, and increase your resources? Absolutely. But all of that will be easier if you remember that your core is good. And you can use what you've got to get what you want, if you stay focused on your mission and trust in yourself and the higher good.

Once you have accepted the fact that you have everything you need to succeed, the first thing to do is to find your mission. Go outdoors into nature, meditate, write in a journal, reflect, and listen to your inner guidance. Ask the big questions: Why are you here? What is your life's purpose?

Wait for the answers to come to you from the center of your being. Then trust in that wisdom and use it to formulate your life's mission. Your mission will emerge from the things that you believe are most important.

Once you have found your mission, take the time to learn more about what you have inside you. Inventory all of your assets—physical, financial, relational, emotional, and spiritual. In each of these areas, you have a distinctive combination of qualities that no one else has. This distinctiveness will help you achieve your goals.

Start from where you are now. You can choose how you want to create the rest of your life by your attitude. You may not be able to control what happens in the outer world, but you can control what happens within you. You can make the choice by the way you respond to what happens to you and around you.

Take one step at a time. When you feel that the world is crowding in on you, breathe deeply and go back to your inner center. Take time to reflect on the deeper implications and meanings of your circumstances. Learn the lessons that your current situation is teaching you. Move forward with the insights that you've learned from your own experience. Observe and absorb the lessons that you see in all of humanity.

When you are feeling stressed, it is easy to be swayed into doing something that seems easier than staying on course toward your mission. But don't let yourself get distracted from your mission by what is most convenient at the time. If your plans and strategies are strong and viable before you embark on them, you will have a high probability of success. Don't hesitate to seek help and support along the way. Be flexible in the development, but focused in the pursuit of your objective.

Organize and structure the steps you are going to take toward your goals. Follow through diligently and enthusiastically. Persevere and don't give up. You can move forward confidently, knowing that you are doing your best and that in itself is worthwhile. It is in the journey that we learn. Regard the desired outcome as a bonus.

Do take time to nurture yourself. You can only do your best if you are 100 percent present and feeling good about yourself. Stay present, be mindful and in the moment. Keep your life centered on your reason for being. Respect and honor yourself and others. It will make you feel good about yourself and it's the right thing to do.

Live each day as if it were your only one. You cannot tell what the future may bring, but if you live each day fully and honestly, then you will have no regrets if it turns out to be your last.

Give thanks for everything you have. If you are bemoaning your lot, be grateful for all the things you don't have that you don't want. Gratitude is an attitude you can cultivate. When you look at life as a half-full glass instead of a half-empty glass, each moment is much more joyful and pleasant. Have fun; share the joy of being alive.

Always remember to follow your passion, tell the truth, take calculated risks, stretch your capabilities, and share. These few short but important phrases will make the difference in how you live your life. You will feel so much more alive and engaged in life when you are committed to being all that you have the potential to be. Follow your dream, regardless of the outcome; you will be at peace if you have tried your best. Otherwise, you will forever wonder if you put off trying until it was too late. Be flexible and stay centered in what you believe. Trust in the right unfoldment of your life.

You are the best advocate for your mission when you truly believe in it. A firm dedication to your purpose will show through in everything you do. When you combine commitment to your mission with respect and mindfulness for the people you are sharing your vision with, charisma and the power to influence are yours. It's yours when you are sharing from your heart.

To increase the chances of success for your dream, determine first the viability of your current strategy to achieve it, and check to make sure that your plan is in line with your purpose. Once you gather and engage the resources necessary, you are on your way to making your plan a reality. It is important to maintain a healthy life balance—to honor your physical and emotional health, spend time with family and friends, and pursue your intellectual interests and spiritual calling. Allow time for laughter and play. You'll feel a lot better and so will everyone around you.

Look at your life as a continuous learning experience. As you embrace new opportunities in your career and everyday life, you will expand your scope and abilities. Explore the unfamiliar and new in your work and in your life; incorporate the attributes you find that can enhance your skills and interactions; take risks—you will learn and advance when you do; keep growing—it keeps you active and alive.

Develop and spend time with mentors. They are your allies and guides as you go through life. You will appreciate the wisdom and encouragement that they offer. From their examples, you may be inspired to mentor others; it is a mutually beneficial relationship that you will enjoy and learn from.

One of the main differences between human beings and animals is that we have the ability to consciously do good. Make a positive difference and it will give back more to you in satisfaction from being a contributor to the world. Incorporate doing good into your work and workplace. Volunteer at a nonprofit organization. Be kind to people and to the environment. Do what you can wherever you are, one step, and one person at a time. Do everything you do with integrity and in line with your life mission and your mind and heart will be at peace. And from that secure place of inner peace, you will know you've already got what you need to get what you want!

Epilogue

It is not the critic who counts; not the man who points out how the strong man stumbles, or where the doer of deeds could have done them better. The credit belongs to the man who is actually in the arena, whose face is marred by dust and sweat and blood; who strives valiantly; who errs and comes short again and again, because there is not effort without error and shortcomings; but who does actually strive to do the deeds; who knows great enthusiasms, the great devotions, who spends himself in a worthy cause; who at the best knows in the end the triumph of high achievement and who at the worst, if he fails, at least he fails while daring greatly, so that his place shall never be with those cold and timid souls who know neither victory nor defeat.

— THEODORE ROOSEVELT

ABOUT MARILYN TAM

MARILYN TAM has accomplished more with her life than she could have ever dreamed. She began life in Kowloon, Hong Kong and has evolved into an influential corporate leader, speaker, consultant, author, and highly respected philanthropist. Raised in a traditional Chinese family, Marilyn received a seed for hope and inspiration from her grandfather, which would continue to bear fruit throughout her life. In her teens, she left Hong Kong, traveling by herself with only two suitcases, for college in the United States. Young Marilyn hoped to find more opportunity in this new, unknown, faraway world.

Marilyn's distinguished professional background includes executive roles at numerous dynamic world-class companies including: May Department Stores, Britannia Sportswear, Miller's Outpost, Nike, Reebok, and Aveda. In each transition, guided by her underlying passion to create change that would make a positive difference in the world, she has gained new insights to living from her four Principles. As she continues to grow, Marilyn has learned that these Principles have served her more and more faithfully. Her growth as a person and as a provider of hope and inspiration is a continuing process. Marilyn has come to realize that a person should never assume that he or she has "arrived," and consequently disregard the very foundations upon which they live.

In the mid 1970s, Marilyn's career began, as she became an executive trainee with May Department Stores California, and quickly rose through the ranks to become the first in her executive training group to be promoted to buyer. Before completing her first year as a buyer, she had earned the responsibility to purchase key products for her department nationally.

By the late 1980s, Marilyn was achieving a global impact. She was instrumental in developing sports performance apparel and accessories for both professional athletes and the general consumer market as the first Vice President of Nike's Apparel and Accessories divisions. Working with Nike's array of world-class athletes and international fabric manufacturers, her team developed new fabrics and accessories to enhance athletic performance. This team led the way in developing coordinated performance apparel, footwear, and accessories, which helped secure Nike's position as the leader in the sports and fitness industry.

Marilyn's leadership as President of Reebok's Apparel and Retail Products Group from 1990 to 1993 was similarly marked by excellence and innovation. Leading the development of Reebok and Rockport retail stores, she succeeded in establishing extremely strong brand identities for her company's products in the midst of a fiercely competitive environment. She led the charge in establishing lightning quick access to critical competitors and market data. Bringing focus and sound plans to the Greg Norman and Reebok Golf Divisions, sales and market share increased greatly under Marilyn's management. She also helped successfully launch the Weebok division of Reebok, a pioneering brand in the children's footwear and activewear markets.

In addition to her corporate leadership, Marilyn became a founding member of the World Peace 2000 Network formed in 1996. She also served for five years on the international board of The Reebok Human Rights Awards, along with former President and 2002 Nobel Peace Prize winner, Jimmy Carter; Special Olympics Chairman Rafer Johnson; and renowned musicians and activists Peter Gabriel and Sting, along with many other distinguished members. Ultimately, she was awarded The Reebok Human Rights Award herself.

The next stage in Marilyn's life brought her to the position of Chief Executive Officer of Aveda Corporation, the organic plant-and flower-based health and beauty company. From 1994 to 1996 she significantly enhanced profitability by developing and implementing successful international expansion strategies and innovative marketing branding initiatives. Her guidance of Aveda positioned the company to be later acquired by Estée Lauder Companies Inc. in a friendly and highly rewarding deal for Aveda. It gave her great satisfaction and pleasure that she was able to play a key role in the growth of a company whose values she strongly believed in. She remains in close friendship with Aveda's founder today.

In February of 2000, Marilyn became President of Fasturn, an eight-person startup company, for which she began consulting just four months earlier. Within a few months of taking on her new position, she and the cofounder of Fasturn had raised over $50 million for this B2B direct procurement software company focusing on the apparel industry. By the spring of 2001, she had grown and established Fasturn's market prominence sufficiently to attract a world-class technology team led by the former Vice President of Oracle Software. The growth in value and market stature of Fasturn under her guidance was an amazing accomplishment considering the demise of many similar companies during that period of time.

Following the successful establishment and transition of the management of Fasturn, Marilyn decided to redirect her undivided attention to what she knew to be her next calling—one that had been in her heart for some time. She would now take the time to write a book, and share with others what she had learned on her journey from colonial Hong Kong to the highest circles of international business and the philanthropic world.

Today, Marilyn's primary work is as the founder and Executive Director of the Us Foundation (www.usfoundation.org), whose mission is to facilitate global action plans and dialogue to address social, economic, and environmental issues. Us Foundation is one of the partners for United Nations' Habitat II (The United Nations Conference on Human Settlements) and has also been nominated for the "Best Practices Award" from the United Nations' Habitat II.

Marilyn is a lifetime member of the Marquis' *Who's Who in the World* and is listed in *Who's Who of American Women*. She also does speaking engagements, and consults with businesses and nonprofits that seek her counsel in developing and enhancing successful, profitable, and healthy organizations. With her unique perspective and global business experience, she is a widely sought after speaker and resource to help organizations learn how to use what they've got to get what they want.

Success has never caused Marilyn to lose touch with the ground beneath her feet, nor her eyes to shift away from necessary work to be done thousands of miles away. Whether directly improving the working conditions of workers in contract factories around the world, developing and conducting seminars to train other entrepreneurs in programs at Universities, or in working with nonprofit organizations, she has maintained a heartfelt commitment to giving something back to others. She is guided by a belief that philanthropy is integral to her career and provides essential balance and relevance to her life's work.

Joining her business acumen with her passion for giving back, Marilyn helps light the way for others who may question whether they have within themselves what they need to succeed and be happy.

READING GROUP GUIDE

Dear Readers:

I'm delighted that your reading group has chosen *How to Use What You've Got to Get What You Want.* It is my fondest wish that this book will motivate you to learn more about your life's purpose, and to use what you already have inside of you to achieve your dreams. I trust that you will find the insights in this book useful in achieving a more gratifying life.

To help you in this quest, I offer below some thought-provoking questions to get your conversations started, and to give you more ways of looking at the issues raised in this book. These questions are designed for a small group meeting one to three hours in length. It is up to you how to handle these questions. You may limit your discussion to one session, or spread it out over several sessions.

If you wish to take each of these Principles to a larger, more in-depth exploration and understanding, I invite you to visit my Website, **www.howtousewhatyouvegot.com**, where you will find additional questions.

QUESTIONS AND DISCUSSION TOPICS

In reading this book, which of the four Principles appeals to you most? Why?

- [TRUTH] **Have you been in a professional situation when you didn't tell the truth? What happened in the end?**

- [PARTNER] **Where and how can you get help to reach cooperation and mutual support on a current project or situation? What do you see as the biggest challenge to achieving this?**

- [MISTAKES] **Overall, do you feel that your level of risk-taking is appropriate for what you are trying to achieve in life? If not, how can you change that?**

- [SWORD] **Can you recall an instance when you didn't do what your research, heart, and instincts told you to do? Were you comfortable with the end results?**

- **What is the biggest obstacle/excuse keeping you from getting what you want?**

Good luck and many blessings to you as you create the life you want.

— MARILYN TAM

For information about public talks and events
given by Marilyn Tam,
please go to
www.howtousewhatyouvegot.com

To book Marilyn Tam
for speaking, consulting, and workshops,
please contact:

Marilyn Tam
c/o Us Foundation
P.O. Box 5780
Santa Barbara, CA 93150
Fax: 805-969-1266
E-mail: info@usfoundation.org

We hope this JODERE GROUP book
has benefited you in your quest
for personal, intellectual, and spiritual growth.

JODERE GROUP is passionate
about bringing new and exciting books, such as
How to Use What You've Got to Get What You Want,
to readers worldwide.
Our company was created
as a unique publishing and multimedia avenue
for individuals whose mission it is
to positively impact the lives of others.
We recognize the strength of an original thought,
a kind word and a selfless act—and the power
of the individuals who possess them.
We are committed to providing the support, passion,
and creativity necessary for these individuals
to achieve their goals and dreams.

JODERE GROUP is comprised of a dedicated and creative
group of people who strive to provide the highest quality
of books, audio programs, online services,
and live events to people who pursue life-long learning.
It is our personal and professional commitment
to embrace our authors, speakers, and readers
with helpfulness, respect, and enthusiasm.

For more information about our products,
authors, or live events, please call
800.569.1002

or visit us on the Web at
www.jodere.com

JODERE
GROUP